Captain
Thomas Posey

and the

7th Virginia
Regiment

Michael Cecere

HERITAGE BOOKS
2007

HERITAGE BOOKS
AN IMPRINT OF HERITAGE BOOKS, INC.

Books, CDs, and more—Worldwide

For our listing of thousands of titles see our website
at
www.HeritageBooks.com

Published 2007 by
HERITAGE BOOKS, INC.
Publishing Division
65 East Main Street
Westminster, Maryland 21157-5026

Other books by the author:

*An Officer of Very Extraordinary Merit: Charles Porterfield and the
American War for Independence, 1775-1780*

In This Time of Extreme Danger: Northern Virginia in the American Revolution

They Are Indeed a Very Useful Corps: American Riflemen in the Revolutionary War

*They Behaved Like Soldiers: Captain John Chilton and the
Third Virginia Regiment, 1775-1778*

International Standard Book Number: 978-0-7884-3584-3

Contents

Maps

Acknowledgements

I am indebted to a number of people for their assistance on this project. Marguerite Knickmeyer, my teaching partner and friend, labored over the manuscript during the Christmas holidays and provided valuable writing help the whole way through. Eric Schnitzer and the national park staff at Saratoga National Battlefield were incredibly generous with their time and research, for which I am eternally grateful. It is always a thrill to visit the park and pick the brains of such knowledgeable and friendly folks.

I'm also grateful to the Revolutionary War re-enacting community. My passion for this period stems from my joy of re-enacting. I'm proud to call many re-enactors on both sides of the war my friend and I look forward to many more years in "the hobby". This is especially true for my friends in the 7th Virginia Regiment. I was welcomed into the unit years ago at Petersburg and have enjoyed every moment. I truly cherish the friendships I've made in the regiment and am proud to call myself a member of the 7th Virginia.

Institutions that provided valuable research help included, the Simpson Library at the University of Mary Washington, the Handley Regional Library in Winchester, Virginia, the David Library in Washington's Crossing, Pennsylvania, and the Library of Congress. Thank you for safe guarding the treasures of the past.

Lastly, I want to thank my wife, Susan, my children, Jenny and Michael, and the rest of my family for their support and encouragement. The phrase, "I have to work on my book" was used a lot last year to avoid many chores, and I suspect that my wife questioned just how much "work" it was when I always seemed to want to do it (rather than the dishes). So thank you Sue, Jenny, Michael, and Mom, Dad, P.J., Matt and Mary Ann, for your love, support, and encouragement.

Chapter One

Virginia Prepares for War

The news arrived in May and swept through Virginia like a thunderclap. The British Ministry had closed Boston Harbor and placed Massachusetts under martial law. Thousands of British troops were en route to Boston to enforce the crackdown. Parliament's long awaited response to the Boston Tea Party had finally arrived.

Although Virginians were not directly affected by these actions, they were deeply troubled by them. In his diary, Colonel Landon Carter expressed the view of many:

> *June 3rd, 1774*
> *Great alarms in the Country. The Parliament of England have declared war against the town of Boston and rather worse; for they have attacked and blocked up their harbour with 3 line of Battle Ships and 6 others, and landed 8 regiments there to subdue them to submit to their taxation; as this is but a Prelude to destroy the Liberties of America, The other Colonies cannot look on the affair but as a dangerous alarm.*[1]

The news disrupted the Virginia House of Burgesses which was meeting in Williamsburg. They had long expected some sort of punitive measure against Boston, but these actions seemed excessive. The Burgesses responded with a symbolic gesture, and proclaimed June 1st, 1774, a day of "Fasting,

---

[1] Jack P. Greene, ed., *The Diary of Landon Carter of Sabine Hall, 1752-1778, Vol. 2,*(Charlottesville: Univ. Press of Virginia, 1965), 817-818

Humiliation, and Prayer," for the people of Boston. Virginia's royal governor, Lord Dunmore, interpreted this action as a challenge to Parliament's authority so he dissolved the assembly. Many of the delegates refused to be intimidated, however, and they met at the Raleigh Tavern to discuss more substantive ways to assist Massachusetts.

Similar discussions occurred throughout the colonies and resulted in a call for a Continental Congress in Philadelphia. Virginia sent seven delegates, including Peyton Randolph, Patrick Henry, George Washington, and Edmund Pendleton to the meeting. They arrived in Philadelphia in early September and immediately began work with the other colonial delegates on a united response to Parliament. They focused on a colonial boycott of British goods.

While the Continental Congress debated the details of this proposal in Philadelphia, numerous Virginia counties moved to protect themselves by forming independent militia companies. Virginians flocked to these units. Large gatherings occurred throughout the colony where British Ministers were hanged in effigy and the King was openly cursed. Nicholas Cresswell was appalled at such behavior. Cresswell was visiting Virginia from England and described the mood of the colony in his diary:

Alexandria, Virginia, October 24th, 1774

Everything here is in the utmost confusion. Committees are appointed to inspect into the Characters and Conduct of every tradesman, to prevent them selling Tea or buying British Manufactures. Some of them have been tarred and feathered, others had their property burnt or destroyed by the populace. Independent Companies are raising in every County on the Continent, appointed Adjutants and train their Men as if they were on the Eve of a War...Subscription is raising in every Colony on the Continent for the relief of the people of Boston. The King is openly cursed, and his authority set at defiance. In short, everything is ripe for rebellion. The New Englanders by their canting, whining, insinuating tricks have persuaded the rest of the Colonies that the Government is going to make absolute slaves of them. [2]

By the spring of 1775, Virginia was ready to explode. In Richmond, the 2nd Virginia Convention was persuaded by the stirring words of Patrick Henry to place the entire colony on a military footing. Three weeks later, Lord Dunmore ignited a firestorm of protest when he transferred a large supply of Virginia's gunpowder from the powder magazine in Williamsburg to a British warship in the James River.

Over a thousand men mustered in Fredericksburg and hundreds of others formed in towns and counties throughout Virginia to march on Williamsburg and demand the return of the powder. Before they arrived, however, a compromise was reached with the governor that briefly defused the crisis. Despite the agreement, tensions remained high, and reports of fighting in Massachusetts convinced many Virginians that a coordinated plot to disarm and oppress the colonies was underway. They continued to organize militia companies and eyed Governor Dunmore with suspicion.

By June, the pressure on Lord Dunmore was so great that he and his family fled to a British warship for protection. Dunmore called on all loyal Virginians to rally around him and suppress the growing rebellion in the colony. When few colonists responded, Dunmore offered freedom to slaves who agreed to fight for him. Even this failed to raise sufficient troops, however.

---

[2] Nicholas Cresswell, *Journal of Nicholas Cresswell, 1774-1777*, (New York: The Dial Press, 1924), 43-44

Virginia

In Williamsburg, the 3rd Virginia Convention also moved to recruit troops. It replaced the independent militia companies with two battalions of regular (full-time) soldiers who served for one year. Each battalion numbered about 500 men and was raised throughout the colony. Additionally, fifteen minute-man battalions, each one also 500 strong, were raised in the colony. These units acted as a ready reserve force and were expected to respond to a crisis at a moment's notice.[3]

This arrangement served Virginia well in its conflict with Lord Dunmore. In the Fall, detachments of regulars and minute-men frequently skirmished with Dunmore's forces near Hampton and Norfolk. In December 1775, six companies of regulars from the 2nd Virginia and four companies of minute-men from the Culpeper battalion combined to defeat Dunmore's troops at the Battle of Great Bridge. The loss forced Dunmore to evacuate Norfolk and flee to the protection of British ships offshore.

Although Virginia's leaders were pleased by this development they were also concerned about Britain's response. In mid-December the Virginia Convention strengthened the colony's defenses. It ordered that,

> *there be immediately raised...six other regiments complete...composed of ten companies of sixty eight men each rank and file, three of which companies in each regiment to consist of riflemen, to act as light infantry....* [4]

---

[3] William Hening, *The Statutes at Large Being a Collection of all the Laws of Virginia, Vol. 9* (Richmond: J & G Cochran, 1821), 10
[4] Ibid., 76

This act quadrupled the number of Virginia's regular troops and doubled their length of service.[5] It also marked a shift in thinking for Virginia's leaders. The bloodshed of 1775 convinced many Virginians to set aside their preference for county militia and place more reliance on full time, "regular" soldiers. The counties still played an important role in recruitment, however. County committees appointed the company officers for the new regiments, (captains, lieutenants, and ensigns). In turn, these officers did most of the recruiting because before they received their commissions, they had to enlist a specified number of men. The quota for captains was 28 men, lieutenants were assigned 21 men, and ensigns, 9 men.[6] Recruits had to be,

> *at least five feet four inches high, healthy, strong made & well limbed, not deaf or Subject to fits....*[7]

After they were sworn into service, the new soldiers received a bounty of twenty shillings.[8] The Convention also agreed to furnish each soldier with,

> *one good musket and bayonet, cartouch box, or pouch and canteen...*[as well as] *a hunting shirt, a pair of leggings, and binding for his hat.*[9]

---

[5] Ibid. 81
[6] Ibid.
[7] Brent Tarter and Robert Scribner, ed., "Orders for Recruiting Regular Soldiers", *Revolutionary Virginia: The Road to Independence, Vol. 6,* (Univ. Press of Virginia, 1983), 15-16
[8] Ibid.
[9] Hening, 81-82

Due to shortages in these items, however, recruits were urged to bring, *"the best gun of any other sort that they can procure,"* as well as a blanket, and, for riflemen, a tomahawk in lieu of a bayonet.[10]

While selection of the company officers and men occurred in the counties, regimental field officers (colonels, lieutenant colonels, and majors) were appointed by the Virginia Convention itself. On January 12th, 1776 the Convention named the field officers for the six new "regular" regiments. Command of the 7th Virginia Regiment went to Colonel William Daingerfield of Spotsylvania County. Alexander McClanahan, of Augusta County, was appointed Lieutenant Colonel and William Nelson of King William County was named Major.[11]

That same day twenty-five year old Thomas Posey was selected by Botetourt County to command a company of riflemen for one of the new regiments.[12] Posey was a newcomer to the Shenandoah Valley (and Botetourt County). He was born and raised in Fairfax County, on a small estate adjacent to Mount Vernon. His father, John, was a friend of George Washington's and served under him in the French and Indian War.[13] In 1769, nineteen year old Thomas Posey took the advice that Washington had given Posey's father two years earlier and set out for the frontier:

---

[10] Ibid.

[11] Tarter and Scribner, "Proceedings of the Fourth Virginia Convention, 12 January, 1776,", *Revolutionary Virginia, Vol. 5,* 391-393

[12] *Thomas Posey's Revolutionary War Journal*, 12 January, 1776, Thomas Posey Papers, Indiana Historical Society Library, Indianapolis, IN (Referred to henceforth as Posey's Journal)

[13] John Thornton Posey, *General Thomas Posey: Son of the American Revolution*, (East Lansing: Michigan State Univ. Press, 1992), 12

there is a large Field before you, an opening prospect in the back Country for Adventurers, where numbers resort to, and where an enterprising Man with very little Money may lay the foundation of a Noble Estate in the New Settlements.[14]

Thomas Posey settled in the frontier community of Staunton and apprenticed at a local saddlery. In 1772, he married Martha Mathews, the eighteen year old daughter of a prominent local merchant. The young couple moved to Fincastle, in Botetourt County, where Posey established his own saddlery shop.[15]

In 1774, with tensions between the colonists and Britain just beginning to rise, Posey left his wife and two children and joined Governor Dunmore's expedition against the Indians. He returned in December to a colony rife with political turmoil. Independent militia companies had formed throughout Virginia and county committees met regularly to discuss affairs. Posey joined the Botetourt County Committee of Correspondence and helped coordinate the County's actions with the newly formed Virginia Committee of Safety.[16] His participation in these activities earned him the respect of County leaders, and when the Virginia Convention called on Botetourt County to furnish a company of riflemen, Posey was chosen to lead it.[17]

Captain Posey had little trouble recruiting his company, and in early March, he was ordered to Gloucester Court House to join the 7th Regiment. The 7th Virginia, as well as the 2nd Virginia, was assigned to protect the area between the York

---

[14] John C. Fitzpatrick, ed., "George Washington to John Posey, 24 June, 1767", *The Writings of George Washington from the Original Manuscripts, 1745-1799*, Vol. 2, (Washington: U.S. Govt. Printing Office, 1931), 458

[15] John Thornton Posey, 18

[16] Ibid. 28

[17] Posey Journal, 12 January, 1776

and Rappahannock Rivers.[18] Captain Posey and his men left Botetourt County on March 20th. He described the journey in his diary,

> [We] *set out upon the march, which was perform'd with great regularity and much good behaviour shown by the soldiers. The conduct was the occasion of a good deal of respect paid by the inhabitants.*[19]

Posey's company arrived at Gloucester on April 1st and was formally incorporated into the 7th Virginia. They were eventually joined by companies from Albemarle (*Capt. Matthew Jouett*), Orange (*Capt. Joseph Spencer*), Cumberland (*Capt. Charles Fleming*), Halifax (*Capt. Nathaniel Cocke*), Essex (*Capt. John Webb*), King William (*Capt. Holt Richeson*), King & Queen (*Capt. Gregory Smith*), Gloucester (*Capt. Charles Tomkies*), and another rifle company from Fincastle (*Capt. Joseph Crockett*). [20] Major William Nelson was the first staff officer to join the regiment at Gloucester Court House. He implemented orders from General Andrew Lewis, in Williamsburg, to conduct daily military drill and adhere to proper military conduct:

> *It is recommended to the Colonels to make their men appear as uniform as possible in their Dress, that their Hatts shall be cut, all cocked in Fashion, that their Hair be likewise cut exactly the same length. When the Regiment are under Arms, the Officers to*

---

[18] Tarter and Scribner, "Virginia Committee of Safety, 10 February, 1776", *Revolutionary Virginia, Vol. 6,* 85
[19] Posey Journal, 20 March, 1776
[20] E.M. Sanchez-Saavedra, *A Guide to Virginia Military Organizations in the American Revolution, 1774-1787.* (Westminster, MD: Willow Bend Books, 1978), 52 and John Frederick Dorman, *Virginia Revolutionary Pension Applications, Volumes 1-52.* (Washington D.C., 1958-95).

appear in their Hunting shirts; the Officers as well as the men to die their shirts in an universal manner. These [details] may appear Trivial, but they are in fact of considerable importance, as they tend to give what is call'd Espirit do Corps, without which Regiments never grow to Reputation.[21]

The 7th Virginia also took measures to secure the area from potential threats. On April 15th, a detachment marched to Urbanna to capture Ralph Wormley, a noted Tory. Major Nelson reported the incident to General Charles Lee, the commander of continental forces in the south:

Mr. Wormely the younger...is now a Prisoner in his Father's house, which is surrounded by Guards, & his own person carefully and constantly watched by two sentinels chosen from among the Cadets of our Regiment. As there was a certain delicacy in the nature of this expedition, I was very nice in the choice of my detachment, & am sure it will give you pleasure to hear that while the Officers of it acted up to the most rigid line of their duty, they never lost sight of politeness & humanity...The situation of Mr. Wormley's house is such as makes me imagine that it will be necessary to reinforce the Party now there, if it is intended to stay any time....[22]

[21] Charles Campbell, *The Orderly Book of that Portion of the American Army stationed at or near Williamsburg, Virginia under the command of General Andrew Lewis, from March 18th, 1776 to August 20th, 1776,* (Richmond, VA: 1860), 13-14

[22] "Major William Nelson to General Charles Lee, 16 April, 1776", *The Lee Papers, Vol. 1,* (Collections of the New York Historical Society, 1871), 429

Such action, as well as the regiment's presence in the area, brought much relief to Gloucester County. However, rumors that the 7th Virginia was about to be transferred from Gloucester worried local residents. On April 22nd, the Gloucester County Committee appealed to General Lee to keep the regiment in the area:

It is with concern that the Committee of Gloster give you this trouble ... The expos'd situation of our County appears to them to merit particular attention: Surrounded almost by a large water, into which a variety of creeks and rivers (perpetually infested with tenders) lead ... it is inconceivable with what facility our enemies might plunder, unless awed by the apprehension of armed men to oppose them. Our inhabitants for some years past accustomed to farming have their plantations in such condition as cannot fail to allure a set of hungry ravagers. However willing to oppose incursions of this sort, they are too much dispersed & too indifferently furnished with arms & ammunition to act with proper effect. It will at once occur to you of how great importance the possession of so fertile & well cultivated a spot wou'd be to the ministerial robbers ... For these reasons we request that you will not withdraw the seventh regiment from Gloster.[23]

---

[23] Tarter and Scribner, "Gloucester County Committee to the Virginia Committee of Safety, 22 April, 1776", *Revolutionary Virginia, Vol. 6*, 441

A compromise was reached at the end of April. On April 31st, five companies from the regiment were sent to Williamsburg under Lieutenant Colonel McClanahan (who joined the regiment on April 19th). Captain Posey's company, however, stayed in Gloucester with the remainder of the regiment. Major Nelson commanded this contingent because the 7th Virginia's commanding officer, Colonel William Daingerfield, still had not joined the unit.[24]

On May 7th, Posey's company was ordered to stand guard at New Point Comfort. It was situated on the Chesapeake Bay, about fifteen miles from Gloucester. Posey recorded in his journal that,

> *I rec'd orders from the comman'g officer to march my company to New Point Comfort where I was to guard against any alarm or surprise made by the enemy upon the troops stationed at the court house, or prevent depredations being commited upon the inhabitants.[25]*

Captain Posey approved of the assignment and took every opportunity to socialize with local residents:

> *This being reather a pleasant situation than otherwise, I spent my time very agreeably; meeting with frequent invitations.[26]*

Two days later, in response to fears that Governor Dunmore might attempt a landing in the area, Posey was ordered to post detachments at the mouth of the East River and at Burton Point, near Gwynn's Island.[27]

---

[24] Posey Journal, 31 April, 1776
[25] Ibid. 7 May, 1776
[26] Ibid.
[27] Ibid. 9 May, 1776

Captain Posey spent the next two weeks inspecting his detachments and socializing with local residents. On May 19th, he, "*recreated at Majr. Smiths where* [he] *dined in company with some very agreeable young ladies.*"[28] The next day, he inspected the guard at Burton's Point and dined with Mr. Armstead, a local resident. After another inspection, Posey, "*got a boat and went to Guins Island to inform* [himself] *of the situation of the ground.*"[29] He added that he was, "*very politely treated by the inhabitants.*"[30]

Gwynn's Island

On May 26th, Captain Posey returned to Gloucester Court House to acquire fresh provisions and report to the commanding officer. "*Upon my arrival,*" noted Posey, "*I found no officer present except two Ensigns.*"[31] At 3:00 p.m. an urgent message arrived from Posey's detachment at Burton Point. Governor Dunmore and his fleet were spotted off Gwynn's Island. Posey recalled,

I immediately sent off an express to the Col. of the regt. who was 3 or 4 miles from camp and in the mean time exerted myself in perading and equipping the regt. for marching. By the time the regt. was ready to march the Col. appeard as also the other officers who were absent. After I rec'd the necessary supplies for my company at New point comfort, I set out with orders to march immediately from the point to join the regt. at Gwyans Island.[32]

---

[28] Posey Journal, 19 May, 1776
[29] Ibid., 21 May, 1776
[30] Ibid.
[31] Ibid. 26 May, 1776
[32] Ibid.

Gwynn's Island & Vicinity

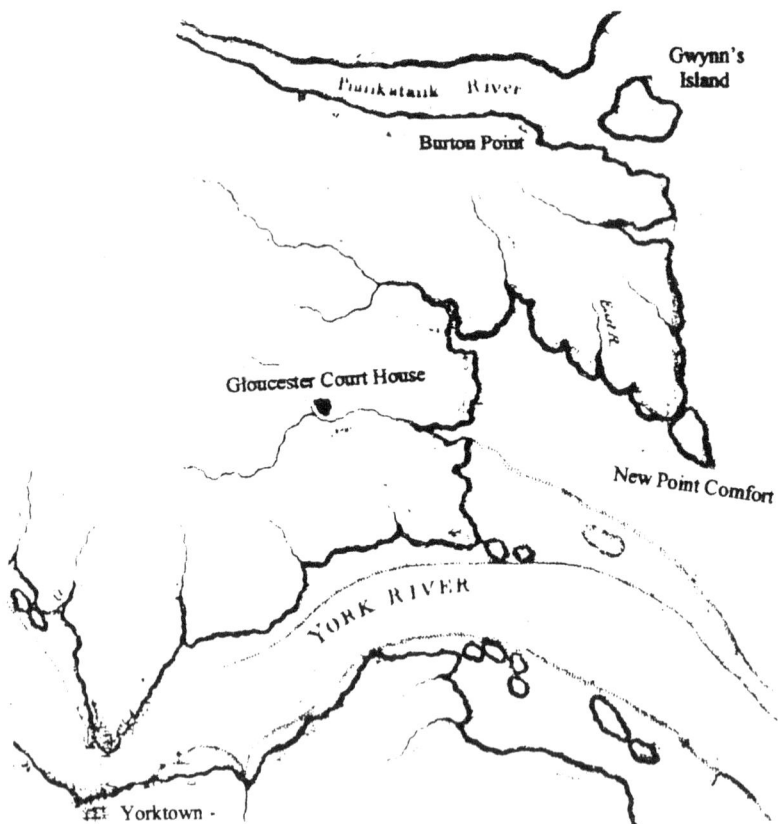

Gwynn's Island

Piankatank River

Burton Point

East R.

Gloucester Court House

New Point Comfort

YORK RIVER

Yorktown

Captain Posey returned to New Point Comfort early the next morning. He immediately assembled his company and marched to Gwynn's Island. When he arrived, he found a chaotic scene:

> *I found a number of the militia assembled, which appear'd to be in the utmost consternation, some running one way, and some another, under no kind of control or regularity.*[33]

Colonel Daingerfield, the commander of the 7th Virginia, had finally joined the regiment and was the highest ranking officer there. He ordered his men, and the militia, to advance closer to the shore to prevent the enemy from landing. Posey observed that,

> *the whole were put in motion, (though I must confess the militia were in very great motion before the orders were given). However, these orders served to put them in something grator; for as soon as we came neare enough for the grape[shot], and cannon shot to whistle over our heads, numbers of the militia put themselves in much quicker motion, and never stoped...to look behind them until they had made the best of there way home.*[34]

Posey was also critical of the regular troops:

> *I cant say that our regulars deserved any great degree of credit for after two or three getting a little blood drawn, they began to skulk and fall flat upon there faces.*[35]

---

[33] Posey Journal, 27 May, 1776
[34] Ibid.
[35] Ibid.

Despite their apprehension, Captain Posey and his men held their ground and endured enemy fire and heavy rain all evening. As the hours passed, they grew more determined to face the enemy. Posey recalled,

we began to grow very firm and only wish them to come into the bushes, where we are certain of beating them.[36]

Rather than attack the mainland, however, Lord Dunmore contented himself with fortifying Gwynn's Island.

The next day, Captain Posey was ordered to man the piquet guard. The post was located on a point of land just 200 yards from the island. A narrow channel of water separated the two sides. Posey recalled that,

Some little time after my being posted, a few shot was fired on the guard, and a tender sent to dislodge us, which brought on a smart fireing; [37]

Posey and his men took shelter behind hastily constructed earthworks and endured the fire. The British resumed a "smart cannonade" the next day, but to little effect. The Virginians answered the steady British bombardment with ineffectual small arms fire.

Although rebel fire had a minimal impact on Dunmore's force, his men suffered greatly from disease. In a letter to Lord Germain, Dunmore described the impact on his troops:

I am extreamly sorry to inform your Lordship that the Fever of which I informed you in my Letter No. 1, has proved a very Malignant one and has carried off an

---

[36] Posey Journal, 27 May, 1776
[37] Ibid. 28 May, 1776

incredible Number of our People, especially the
Blacks, had it not been for this horrid disorder, I am
Satisfied I should have had two thousand Blacks, with
whom I should have no doubt of penetrating into the
heart of the Colony...There was not a ship in the fleet
that did not throw one, two, or three or more dead
overboard every night.[38]

The Virginians were well aware of Dunmore's losses.
General Andrew Lewis, the commander of Virginia's
Continental forces (in General Charles Lee's absence),
reported daily sightings of bodies to General Lee. *"A Great*
Mortality among the Enemy, some both white and black, are
discovered floating every day"[39] Captain Posey also noted the
enemy's problems and recorded in his diary that, *"a number of*
dead bodies were found upon our shore."[40] Although
Dunmore's force suffered terribly from smallpox and fever,
they were still glad to be on land. There was plenty of fresh
provision on the island, and they were relatively secure from
attack.[41]

Captain Posey and his fellow Virginians worked hard to
change that, however. Despite frequent enemy gunfire the
Virginians made steady progress on their earthworks and
artillery battery. General Lewis informed General Lee of
developments:

---

[38] William Clark, ed., "Lord Dunmore to Lord Germain, 26 June, 1776",
Naval Documents of the American Revolution, Vol. 5, (Washington:
1970), 756
[39] "Brigadier General Andrew Lewis to Major General Charles Lee, 12
June, 1776", *Naval Documents of the American Revolution, Vol. 5* 501
[40] Posey Journal, 7 June, 1776
[41] Lord Dunmore to Lord Germain, 26 June, 1776", *Naval Documents of
the American Revolution, Vol. 5*, 756

17

I have ordered several Pieces of Cannon at Gloucester Town to be mounted, which the workmen are about, in order to have them mounted opposite the Enemy and if possible, to prevent some small armed Vessels getting out which lie between the mainland and the Island. I have sent under the Command of Col. Mercer three companies to reinforce Col. Dangerfield's Battalion.... [42]

It was another three weeks before the Virginians were ready to attack Dunmore's force. In the interim, they contented themselves with sniping at British ships in the channel. In one incident, the Virginians were able to seize a small ship loaded with spirits. Posey recalled,

We took a small sailing vessel from the enemy, she was loaded with rum, brandy, whisky, and sundry other things. The engagement lasted near half an hour warmly kept up on both sides until at length by the loss of almost all her crew she was obligated to strike. [43]

General Lewis also described the attack in a letter to General Lee:

Our men took a small sloop endeavouring to get out of the Narrows between the Island and our breastwork. She having run a Ground, a few men in two small Canoes boarded her, five men who were all her crew endeavoured to escape by swimming – three of which were shot from the shoar and sunk. Two hogsheads of Brandy, ½ Ditto of Rum, some tools

---

[42] "Brigadier General Lewis to Major General Lee, 12 June, 1776", *The Lee Papers, Vol. 1*, 63

[43] Posey Journal, 9 June, 1776

and ropes...were taken out for the use of our Troops
there, who were in need of the brandy and rum, as
the water is very bad. [44]

The British intensified their bombardment of the Virginians in the latter half of June. Besides slowing the work of the fatigue parties a bit, the bombardment had little effect.

The situation changed on the morning of July 9th, when the Virginians completed a battery consisting of two eighteen pound cannon and a mortar. It was located directly across from the British camp and was revealed to the enemy in dramatic fashion. Captain Posey described what happened:

At ten o clock orders were given by Genl. Lewis to
open the whole of the batteries, two of which were
opposite the enemies encampment and the main
battery within a few hundred yards of the fleet. The
fireing was kept up in a very regular manner from the
whole of our works for near two hours; during which
time they received great damage.... [45]

General Lewis reportedly aimed and fired the first cannon at Lord Dunmore's ship, the *Dunmore.* The eighteen pound ball crashed through its stern. Another round destroyed Dunmore's cabin, killed an aide, and slightly wounded the Governor. More cannonballs landed amidst the British camp and created panic among the men.[46]

---

[44] "General Lewis to General Lee, 12 June, 1776", *Lee Papers, Vol. 1,* 64
[45] Posey Journal, 9 July, 1776
[46] Peter Wrike, *The Governor's Island,* (Gwynn, VA: The Gwynn's Island Museum, 1993), 79

With Dunmore's troops in disarray, the Virginians scrambled to procure boats to cross the channel and press the enemy. Captain Posey described what happened:

Upon the enemies receiving this very unexpected stroke, they gave immediate orders to evacuate the Island. On the discovery of which, orders were given to cross into the island and endeavour to harass the enemy in the rear. Col. McClannahan was directed to take command of about 200 men for the afore said purpose.[47]

A lack of boats delayed this crossing until the next morning. By then, Dunmore and his men had evacuated the island and returned to their ships. Captain Posey was one of the first Virginians on the island and described the landing in his diary:

crossed into the Island but no fighting ensued except a few shot. By one oclock the whole of the enemy had evacuated and embarked...I cannot help observeing, that I never saw more distress in my life, than what I found among some of the poor deluded Negroes which they could not take time, or did not chuse to cary off with them, they being sick. Those that I saw, some were dying, and many calling out for help; and throughout the whole Island we found them stre'd about, many of them torn to pieces by wild beasts – great numbers of the bodies having never been buried.[48]

---

[47] Posey Journal, 9 July, 1776
[48] Ibid. 10 July, 1777

British losses at Gwynn's Island are difficult to ascertain. Captain Posey estimated, *"that at least 4 or 500 negroes lost their lives."*[49] Posey added that another 150 [white] soldiers were also lost.[50] The vast majority of these deaths occurred prior to the attack as a result of disease. Such losses significantly hampered the effectiveness of Dunmore's force and explain his feeble response to the attack.

The events at Gwynn's Island exasperated Lord Dunmore. His men were weak from illness and demoralized by defeat and there was little hope of assistance from Britain. By mid-August Dunmore had had enough and he abandoned his efforts to regain Virginia. Half of his force sailed to St. Augustine, Florida and the other half sailed, with him, to New York.

Captain Posey and most of the 7th Virginia returned to Gloucester Courthouse a few days after the battle. A small guard was left on Gwynn's Island to keep watch for the enemy.[51] A week later Colonel Daingerfield resigned his commission, leaving Lieutenant Colonel McClanahan in command.[52] In mid-August word arrived of Indian unrest on the frontier. Posey sought permission to return to Botetourt County to defend his home and family. His request was denied, and he was ordered to take command of two companies and return to Gwynn's Island.[53] The rest of the 7th Virginia encamped at Gloucester Court House and Yorktown.

---

[49] Posey Journal, 10 July, 1776
[50] Ibid.
[51] Ibid., 11 July, 1776
[52] Ibid., 17 July, 1776
[53] Ibid., 25 August, 1776

Three weeks later, Captain Posey received permission to return home.[54]

When he arrived, he discovered that the reports were false. The frontier was calm and his family was safe. He stayed with them for a month and departed on October 15th. When Posey returned to the regiment he found the 7th Virginia comfortably settled in winter quarters near Williamsburg. He recalled that,

During the time of our stay the inhabitants endeavoured to make it pass off as agreeable as possible. [55]

Their comfortable arrangement was soon disturbed by grim news from the north. General Washington's army had been forced out of New York and chased across New Jersey. In a matter of months, his 20,000 man army shrank to a few thousand. Ill clad and poorly supplied, they sought refuge on the west bank of the Delaware River.

A ray of hope emerged with Washington's bold action at Trenton and Princeton. The British recoiled from these attacks and withdrew to the coastline of New Jersey. Washington responded by establishing winter quarters in the mountains of central New Jersey. Despite their aggressive victories at Trenton and Princeton the American army remained weak. General Washington urgently pressed the states to send reinforcements and supplies. On January 9th, the 7th Virginia received orders to join Washington's army and following a week of preparation they commenced their march northward. [56]

---

[54] Posey Journal, 10 September, 1776
[55] Ibid.
[56] Ibid., 16 January, 1776

Chapter Two

1777

While the 7th Virginia marched north via Fredericksburg and Alexandria, Captain Posey received permission for another visit with his family. He planned to rejoin the regiment in Baltimore or Philadelphia, and after a ten day reunion with his loved ones, he set off to do so. On February 19th, Posey arrived in Frederick, Maryland, where he was inoculated for smallpox.[1] The process normally took three to four weeks to complete and Posey endured it uneventfully. The rest of his regiment was inoculated on their way north, some in Alexandria and Baltimore, and the bulk in Philadelphia.[2]

Captain Posey rejoined the regiment on March 15th, in Philadelphia, and spent the next three weeks, *"clothing the regt. and preparing for our march to join the main army."*[3] On April 4th, the 7th Virginia crowded into small boats and sailed up the Delaware River to Trenton. They arrived three days later and marched to Middlebrook, arriving on April 12th.[4] The next day, Posey and his men awoke to the sound of combat. The battle of Boundbrook erupted just three miles from their encampment, and the 7th Virginia was called upon to help cover the army's retreat. The enemy did not aggressively pursue, however, and the situation soon stabilized.[5]

---

[1] Posey Journal, 9 February, 1777
[2] See: John Frederick Dorman, *Virginia Revolutionary Pension Applications*, Vol. 7 Thomas Blacknall, 35; Vol. 16 Warren Cash, 84; and Vol. 34, John Estes, 49
[3] Posey Journal, 15 March, 1777
[4] Ibid., 4-12 April, 1777
[5] Ibid.

Captain Posey and the 7th Virginia spent the next few weeks on alert, very close to the enemy. Posey noted in his journal that,

Here we continued to do duty, which was rather fatigueing for our numbers, as we had a very large extent of country to guard and the enemy in possession of a great many advantageous posts within a small distance of us.[6]

With the approach of the campaign season, General Washington re-organized the army. On May 11th, he brigaded the 7th Virginia with the 3rd, 11th, and 15th Virginia regiments and placed General William Woodford in command.[7] General Washington instructed Woodford to keep the brigade together and exercise the men as much as possible:

The necessity of occupying so many Posts, as we at present do, will prevent your drawing the Brigade into compact order, till further orders; but the Regiments should be kept as much together, as the nature of the Service will admit...Whenever your Brigade can be drawn together, you should make them practice, as much as possible, the Evolutions (as more essential than the Manual exercise)...."[8]

Within a week of these instructions, the 7th Virginia found itself on the parade ground with Colonel Daniel Morgan's 11th

---

[6] Posey Journal, 13 April, 1777

[7] "General Orders for 11 May, 1777" and "General Washington to General Woodford, 10 May, 1777", *The Writings of George Washington, Vol. 8,* 41 ; 40

[8] "Washington to Woodford, 10 May, 1777", *The Writings of George Washington, Vol. 8,* 40

Virginia regiment.[9] A week later, Captain Posey commented on the marked improvement of the troops, *"we began to appear very formidable; we had possession of a very strong ground"*[10]

Posey's involvement with the 7th Virginia soon drew to a temporary close, however. In June he was selected as one of eight captains to command a company of riflemen in Colonel Daniel Morgan's new Rifle Corps. Posey's rifle company from the 7th Virginia joined him in this corps and remained under his command.

Morgan's Rifle Corps

Captain Posey and his men were undoubtedly proud of their selection to this special unit. General Washington formed the rifle corps to address the need for light infantry and scouts. He informed Colonel Morgan that,

> *The corps of Rangers newly formed and under your command, are to be considered as a body of light infantry, and are to act as such, for which reason they will be exempted from the common duties of the line.*[11]

---

[9] *Orderly Book of Major William Heth of the Third (sic) Virginia Regiment, May 15 – July 1, 1777*
Note: This orderly book is incorrectly titled and is actually the orderly book of Daniel Morgan's 11th Virginia Regiment.
(Accessed thru the internet at: www.ls.net/~newriver/va/heth.htm)
[10] Posey Journal, 24 May, 1776
[11] Chase, Philander D. ed, "General Washington to Colonel Morgan, 13 June, 1777", *The Papers of George Washington*: Revolutionary War Series, Vol. 10, (Charlottesville: Univ. Press of Virginia, 2000), 31 (Forthwith referred to as the Papers of George Washington)

As riflemen, Morgan's troops held both an advantage and a disadvantage over the enemy. In an age when most soldiers used smoothbore muskets, with an effective range of 50 to 100 yards, experienced riflemen could consistently hit their mark at more than 200 yards. The advantage that rifles had in accuracy, however, was somewhat negated by their lower rate of fire. Musket-men, using pre-rolled cartridges, which easily fit in their smoothbore barrels, could fire up to four rounds a minute. Riflemen, on the other hand, typically measured each charge from a powder horn. Furthermore, to ensure that the bullet would spin, and thus be more accurate when firing, it was wrapped in a greased cloth patch to produce a very tight fit in the grooved rifle barrels. This made it difficult to ram the bullet to the bottom of the barrel and resulted in riflemen taking two to three times longer to load their weapons. Another disadvantage of rifles was that, in most cases, bayonets could not be attached to them. Thus, in close combat situations, riflemen found themselves at a distinct disadvantage to their bayonet wielding enemy. To compensate for their lack of bayonets, General Washington procured spears for the riflemen, but they proved too cumbersome to handle and were soon disregarded.

Morgan's corps comprised riflemen from the whole army (500 in all) and the unit was immediately put to use. On the day of its formation, General Washington ordered Colonel Morgan to,

> *take post at Van Vechten's Bridge, and watch, with very small scouting parties (to avoid fatiguing your men too much...) the enemy's left flank...In case of any movement of the enemy, you are instantly to fall upon their flanks, and gall them as much as possible, taking especial care not to be surrounded, or to have your retreat to the army cut off.*[12]

---

[12] Ibid.

The next day the rifle corps skirmished with the enemy. General Washington described the encounter in a letter to General John Sullivan:

The Enemy have advanced a party; said to be two thousand, as far as Van Ests Mill upon Millstone River. They have been skirmishing with Colo. Morgans Riflemen but have halted on a piece of high ground....[13]

Washington ordered Colonel Morgan to maintain contact with the enemy:

His Excellency desires you will continue to keep out your active parties carefully watching every motion of the enemy; and have your whole body in readiness to move without confusion, and free from danger....[14]

The British held their position for nearly a week, and Morgan's riflemen engaged them in daily skirmishes. When the enemy finally withdrew, Morgan's rifle corps pursued them all the way to Piscataway. Washington noted that, *"In the pursuit, Colo. Morgans Rifle Men exchanged several sharp Fires with the Enemy, which it is imagined did them considerable execution."* [15] Captain Posey described one of the engagements in his biography:

The [rifle] regiment was posted in a thick wood somewhat swampy near the rode, & when the main body of the enemy passed, & the rear guard came on,

---

[13] "General Washington to General Sullivan, 14 June, 1777", *The Papers of George Washington, Vol. 10*, 40

[14] "Richard Meade to Daniel Morgan, 16 June, 1777", *The Papers of George Washington, Vol. 10*, 40

[15] "General Washington to John Hancock, 22 June, 1777", *The Papers of George Washington, Vol. 10*, 104-105

Morgan ordered the regiment to attack and indeavour to cut it off. The order was promptly obeyed, & the action was warmly contested on both sides; in the course of the action Capt. Posey was ordered with his company across a causeway, being through a considerable swamp to gain the front of the enemy which was promptly executed & a sharp conflict took place, but the light Infantry of the enemy surrounded his company, and was near cutting him off he perceiving his situation ordered a well directed fire upon a particular part of the enemy, which opened a passage for him to retreat through. Through the course of the action the regiment sustained considerable loss in killed & wounded, the enemy suffered very considerably, tho' the highest loss fell upon Capt. Posey's company.[16]

In a letter to Joseph Reed, General Washington emphasized the enemy's loss:

I fancy the British Grenadiers got a pretty severe peppering yesterday by Morgan's Riffle Corp – they fought it seems a considerable time within the distance of, from twenty to forty yards...more than a hundd of them must have fallen.[17]

Four days later, General Howe renewed his efforts to draw Washington out of his fortified lines with a sudden march towards the American left flank. This movement surprised the Americans and was nearly a disaster for the rifle corps.

---

[16] *"A Short Biography of the Life of Governor Thomas Posey,"* Thomas Posey Papers, Indiana Historical Society Library, Indianapolis, IN (Referred to henceforth as Posey's Biography)

[17] "General Washington to Joseph Reed, 23 June, 1777", *The Papers of George Washington, Vol. 10,* 115

Captain John Chilton of the 3rd Virginia Regiment, described what happened:

> *Col. Morgan with the Rifle Regmt. was on the Mattuchin lines at the time and our main army had come down into the Plains. The Enemy unexpectedly stole a march in the night of the 25th and had nearly surrounded Morgan before he was aware of it. He with difficulty saved his men and baggage and after a retreat, rallied his men and sustained a heavy charge until reinforced by Major Genl. Ld. Stirling, who gave them so warm a reception that they were obliged to retreat so precipitately that it had like to have become a rout. But being strongly reinforced he [Stirling] was obliged to retreat with the loss of 2 pieces of Artillery.*[18]

Although the American advance parties, including Morgan's corps, were forced to retreat, the main American position remained secure. General Howe, discouraged at his failure to draw the American army away from its fortified position and into an open engagement, withdrew to Amboy to develop a new plan of attack.

In early July, General Washington received reports that a large British force had boarded ships in New York. Their destination was both a mystery and a concern to Washington, who speculated that the British were heading up the Hudson River to join General John Burgoyne's army. Burgoyne was marching south from Canada with 7,000 men, in an effort to split New England from the rest of the states. If General Howe's force united with Burgoyne, they would overwhelm

---

[18] Lyon Tyler, "John Chilton to his brother, 29 June, 1777", in "The Old Virginia Line in the Middle States During the American Revolution," *Tyler's Quarterly Historical and Genealogical Magazine, Vol. 12,* (Richmond, VA: Richmond Press Inc., 1931), 118

New Jersey

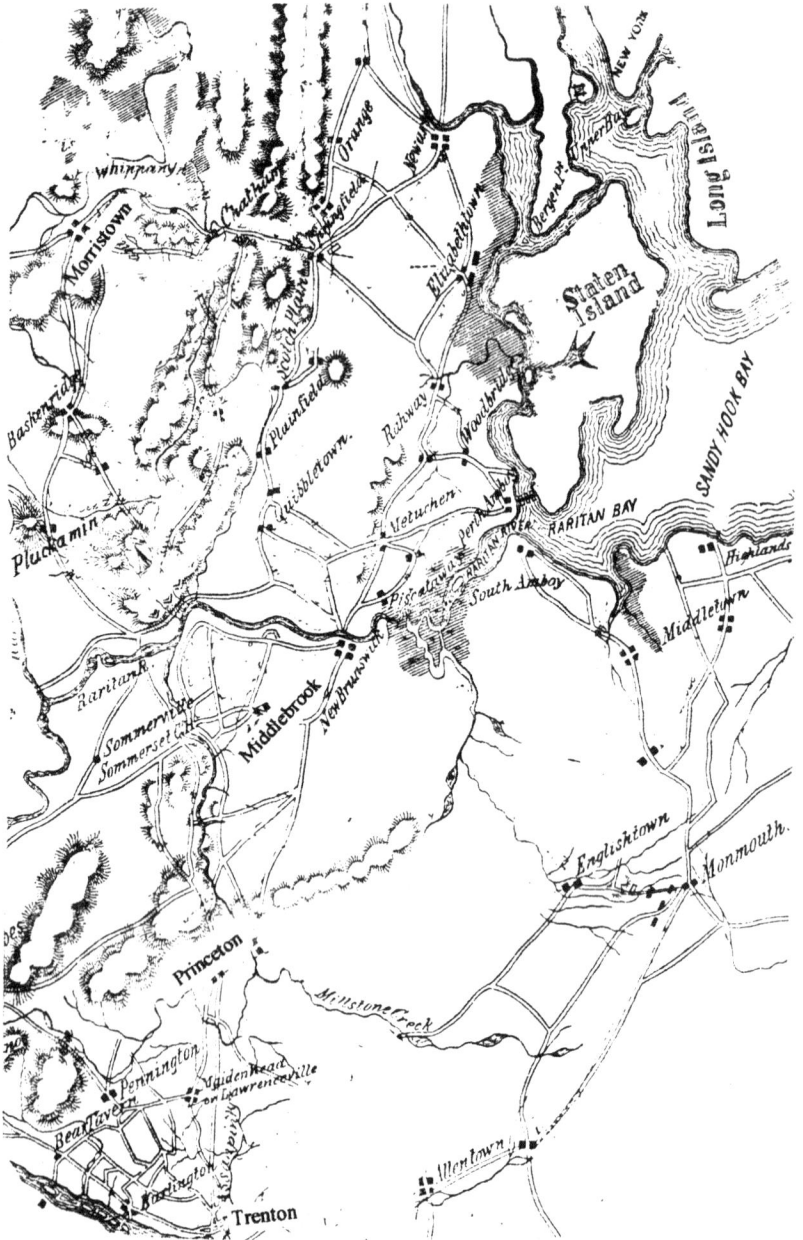

General Philip Schuyler's small American army in New York. Washington set the main army in motion and headed north. They arrived in Chester, New York on July 23rd, but quickly turned around and commenced a forced march back to Philadelphia.[19] The reason for the sudden turnabout was a report that the British fleet was actually off the coast of New Jersey and heading south. If this were true, then General Washington was dangerously out of position to defend Philadelphia. With the summer sun blazing down on them, the 7th Virginia and the rest of the American army marched south, covering seventy miles in three days.[20] Captain John Chilton of the 3rd Virginia described the ordeal in his diary:

> *no victuals to eat as the (march) of last night was so late that nothing could be cooked, no wagons allowed to carry our Cooking utensils, the soldiers were obliged to carry their Kettles, pans, &c. in their hands, Clothes and provisions on their backs...As our march was a forced one & the Season extremely warm, the victuals became putrid with sweat & heat - the Men badly off for Shoes, many being entirely barefoot.*[21]

The rest of army, including the 7th Virginia and Morgan's rifle corps, experienced similar conditions.

By August, Washington's army was encamped only a day's march from Philadelphia. They remained there for nearly three weeks and welcomed the opportunity to rest. The reason for the long halt was General Washington's uncertainty about the enemy's location. The British fleet had disappeared over the horizon and a lack of reliable intelligence caused General Washington a lot of anxiety. He had no way of knowing that

---

[19] Diary of Capt. Chilton, 23-25 July, 1777, in *Tyler's Quarterly*, 284
[20] Diary of Capt. Chilton, 26-28 July, 1777, in *Tyler's Quarterly*, 285
[21] Diary of Capt. Chilton, 27 July, 1777, in *Tyler's Quarterly*, 286

the fleet was stuck off the coast, unable to reach Chesapeake Bay due to contrary winds. He impatiently waited for news of its location.

The Rifle Corps Heads North

General Washington was concerned with more than the whereabouts of General Howe's army. Alarming news from New York about General Burgoyne's advance from Canada and disturbing reports of Indian atrocities, which spread terror throughout the region, worried him. General Schuyler, the commander of American forces in New York, complained to Washington that fear of the Indians had infected his troops:

The most unaccountable panic has seized the Troops that was ever heard of – A few shot from a small party of Indians has more than once thrown them into the greatest Confusion – The Day before Yesterday three hundred of our Men...came running in, being drove by a few Indians, certainly not more than fifty. [22]

General Schuyler also lamented the lack of troops to oppose the enemy:

We have not one Militia from the Eastern States & under forty from this – Can it therefore any longer be a matter of Surprise that we are obligated to give way and retreat before a vastly superior force daily increasing in numbers.... [23]

---

[22] "General Philip Schuyler to General George Washington, 1 August, 1777", *The Papers of George Washington, Vol.* 10, 482-483
[23] "General Philip Schuyler to General George Washington, 13 August, 1777", *The Papers of George Washington, Vol.* 10, 606

General Washington wanted to assist Schuyler, but with Howe's army hovering somewhere off the coast, he was unable to send a large reinforcement. He could send a countermeasure to the Indians, however, and on August 16th, Washington reluctantly ordered Colonel Morgan's rifle corps to join the northern army in New York:

After you receive this you will march, as soon as possible, with the corps under your command, to Peekskill, taking with you all the baggage belonging to it. When you arrive there, you will take directions from General Putnam, who, I expect, will have vessels provided to carry you to Albany. The approach of the enemy in that quarter has made a further reinforcement necessary. I know of no corps so likely to check their progress, in proportion to its number, as that under your command. I have great dependence on you, your officers and men, and I am persuaded you will do honor to yourselves, and essential services to your country.[24]

General Washington explained his decision to send the rifle corps northward to General Israel Putnam:

The people in the Northern army seem so intimidated by the Indians, that I have determined to send up Colonel Morgan's corps of riflemen, who will fight them in their own way.[25]

Washington also expressed his confidence in the abilities of the rifle corps to New York Governor George Clinton:

---

[24] "General Washington to Colonel Daniel Morgan, 16 August, 1777", *The Papers of George Washington, Vol. 10,* 641
[25] "General Washington to General Israel Putnam, 16 August, 1777", *The Papers of George Washington, Vol. 10,* 642

I am forwarding as fast as possible, to join the Northern army, Colonel Morgan's corps of riflemen, amounting to about five hundred. These are all chosen men, selected from the army at large, well acquainted with the use of rifles, and with that mode of fighting, which is necessary to make them a good counterpoise to the Indians; and they have distinguished themselves on a variety of occasions, since the formation of the corps, in skirmishes with the enemy. I expect the most eminent services from them, and I shall be mistaken if their presence does not go far towards producing a general desertion among the savages.[26]

Colonel Morgan's orders were slightly adjusted during his march to New York. Congress removed General Schuyler from command of the northern army and installed General Horatio Gates in his place. Morgan was instructed to report directly to General Gates, who was encamped with the army north of Albany.

Gates was very pleased to hear of the rifle corps' transfer and expressed his sentiments in a letter to General Washington:

I cannot sufficiently thank your Excellency for sending Colonel Morgan's corps to this army; they will be of the greatest service to it, for until the late successes this way, I am told the army were quite panic-struck by their Indians, and their Tory and Canadian assassins in Indian dresses.[27]

---

[26] "General Washington to George Clinton, 16 August, 1777", *The Papers of George Washington, Vol. 10*, 634-636

[27] "General Gates to General Washington, 22 August, 1777", *The Papers of George Washington, Vol. 11*, 38

A week later, General Gates wrote to Colonel Morgan, who was near Albany:

> *I had much satisfaction in being acquainted by General Washington of your marching for this department. I have ...ordered Colonel Lewis ...at Albany, to provide you, immediately upon your landing, with carriages for your baggage, and whatever may be necessary; tents, and a camp equipage, I conclude you have brought with you.*[28]

The situation began to improve for the Americans, even before Morgan's arrival. The successful defense of Fort Stanwix and the stunning victory at Bennington, where 2,000 New Hampshire and Vermont militia commanded by General John Stark overwhelmed a 700 man foraging party from Burgoyne's army, significantly improved American morale. By September, General Gates's army surpassed Burgoyne's in size, and a new sense of optimism gripped the Americans.[29] This feeling was heightened with the arrival of Morgan's corps.

Unfortunately, three months of active service, and the long march north, took a toll on the rifle corps. Less than 400 riflemen arrived with Colonel Morgan. Over 100 men were absent due to illness.[30] General Gates partially alleviated

---

[28] James Graham, "General Gates to Colonel Morgan, 29 August, 1777", *The Life of General Daniel Morgan*, (Bloomingburg, NY: Zebrowski Historical Services, 1993), 138

[29] Charles H. Lesser, ed. "A General Return of the Continental Troops Under the Command of Major General Horatio Gates, 7 September, 1777 (Gates Papers) in *The Sinews of Independence: Monthly Strength Reports of the Continental Army*, (Chicago: The Univ. of Chicago Press, 1976), 49

[30] General James Wilkinson, "A Return of Colonel Morgan's detachment of Riflemen, 3 September, 1777", *Memoirs of My Own Times, Vol. 1* (Philadelphia: Abraham Small, 1816) Appendix C Reprinted by AMS Press Inc., :NY, 1973

Morgan's manpower shortage by drafting fifteen of the most hardy musket-men from each regiment to serve in a light infantry corps.[31] They were led by Major Henry Dearborn and attached to Colonel Morgan's command.

The addition of 250 hand-picked musket-men with bayonets, greatly enhanced the fighting capabilities of Morgan's corps. This undoubtedly pleased Colonel Morgan, as did the news that the light troops' commander was an old acquaintance of his from the 1775 Quebec expedition. These two officers, Colonel Morgan and Major Dearborn, played a crucial role in the battles of Saratoga, and Captain Posey and his riflemen from the 7th Virginia, fought right alongside them.

---

[31] "General Gates to Colonel Morgan, 29 August, 1777", in Graham, *The Life of General Daniel Morgan*, 138

Chapter Three

Saratoga

With a counter measure to Burgoyne's Indians finally in camp, and an influx of reinforcements swelling the ranks, General Gates decided to advance towards the enemy. On September 7th, the army marched north. Five days later, they took possession of Bemis Heights, an excellent defensive position overlooking the Hudson River. General Gates decided to make his stand there, and the army commenced to fortify the position and await the enemy.

General Burgoyne, after nearly a month's stay at Fort Miller to gather sufficient provision, resumed his march to Albany on September 13th. The British crossed the Hudson River and camped near Saratoga, just eleven miles from Bemis Heights. They continued southward on September 15th, but were delayed by the destruction of a number of bridges. In the evening, small parties of Americans probed their encampment and alarmed the sentries.[1] Captain Posey and his men probably participated in some of these activities. Years later Posey recalled that,

> *After the* [rifle] *regiment joined* [the American army] *it was ordered on the enemies lines, where it continued to harass the enemy at all times....*[2]

---

[1] James Baxter, ed. *The British Invasion from the North: Digby's Journal of the Campaigns of Generals Carleton and Burgoyne from Canada, 1776-1777*, (New York: Da Capo Press, 1970), 267 (Henceforth referred to as Digby Journal)
[2] Posey Biography

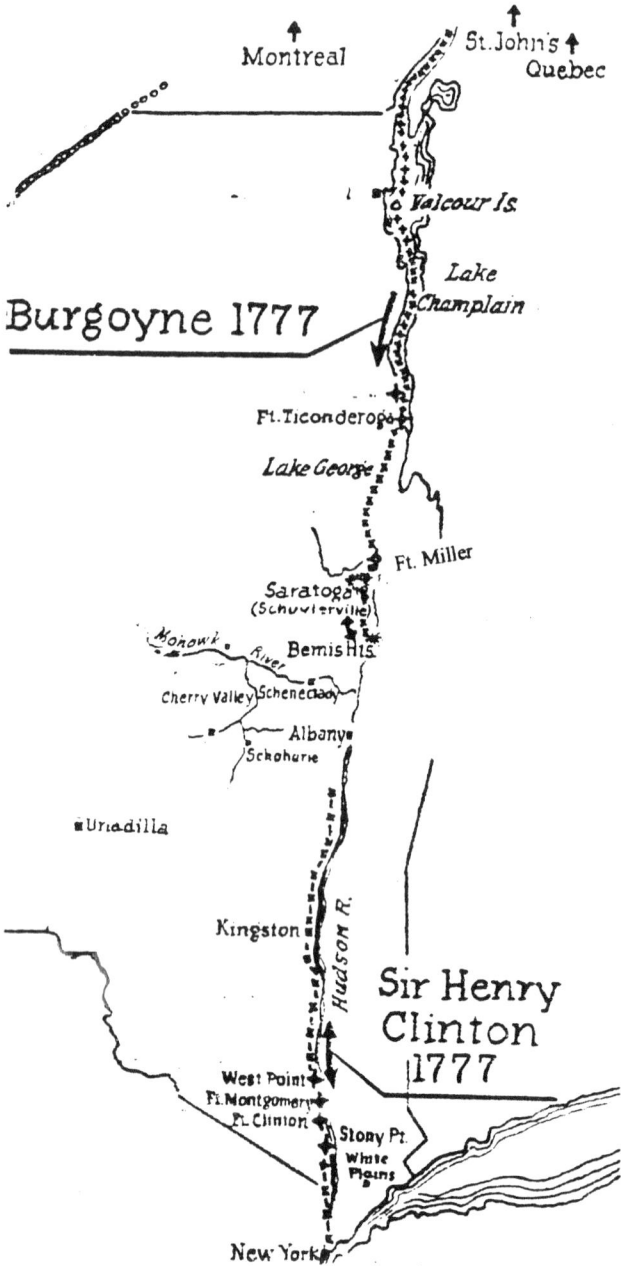

New York

Montreal ↑   St. John's ↑ Quebec

Valcour Is.

Lake Champlain

Burgoyne 1777

Ft. Ticonderoga

Lake George

Ft. Miller

Saratoga (Schuylerville)

Mohawk River   Bemis Hts.

Cherry Valley   Schenectady

Albany

Schoharie

▪ Unadilla

Kingston

Hudson R.

Sir Henry Clinton 1777

West Point
Ft. Montgomery
Ft. Clinton   Stony Pt.
   White Plains

New York

Although the constant alarms disturbed the British, they remained confident of success. On September 17th, they marched to within four miles of the American camp. The next day, skirmishes occurred on the fringe of the British lines. In one incident a party of British soldiers and camp followers, foraging for potatoes, was surprised by a party of Americans. The British viewed the encounter with disdain because the foragers were unarmed, yet at least thirteen were shot by the Americans. A British officer noted in his journal that,

> *Such cruel and unjustifiable conduct can have no good tendency, while it serves greatly to increase hatred and a thirst for revenge.*[3]

Once again, General Burgoyne's army spent the night under arms and on edge. Their opportunity for revenge was only hours away.

Battle of Freeman's Farm

September 19th dawned brisk and foggy, with the opposing armies only a few miles apart, yet neither side was fully aware of their opponent's troop disposition. This did not stop General Burgoyne, however. He was determined to reach Albany, and the American army was in his way.

Burgoyne decided to take the initiative and attack. He divided his army into three columns. The left column, commanded by General von Riesdel, numbered 1,600 men

---

[3] Sydney Jackman ed. *With Burgoyne from Quebec: An Account of the Life at Quebec and of the Famous Battle at Saratoga,* (Toronto: Macmillan of Canada, 1963), 172
Note: First published as volume one of *Travels Through the Interior Parts of North America*, by Thomas Anburey   (Henceforth referred to as Anburey)

(mostly German) and marched along the river road.[4]   It included most of the artillery and a large baggage train protected by the 47th British regiment.   General Burgoyne's right column, commanded by General Simon Fraser, was the largest British force, with 2,400 men.[5] Burgoyne expected the right column to screen the right flank of the army's advance and gain the enemy's left flank. To do so, Fraser marched nearly three miles west, away from the river, and then swung south towards the Americans.

General Burgoyne marched with the center column which moved in a diagonal direction from the river.   It totaled 1,500 men from the 9th, 20th, 21st, and 62nd British regiments and was commanded by General James Hamilton.   Four pieces of artillery were also part of this column.[6]

The three columns began their march around 9:00 a.m. and were immediately spotted by American pickets on the east side of the river. Word reached the American camp that the enemy was on the move. General Gates ordered Colonel Morgan's light corps (riflemen and light infantry) to reconnoiter the area north of camp. According to Colonel James Wilkinson, an aide to General Gates, the General,

ordered Colonel Morgan to advance his corps, who was instructed, should he find the enemy approaching, to hang on their front and flanks, to retard their march, and cripple them as much as possible. [7]

---

[4] John Luzader, *Decision on the Hudson: The Battles of Saratoga*, (Eastern National, 2002), 41

[5] Ibid.

[6] Richard M. Ketchum, *Saratoga,: Turning Point of America's Revolutionary War*, (NY: Holt & Co., 1997), 357

[7] General James Wilkinson, *Memoirs of My Own Times*, Vol. 1, (Philadelphia: Abraham Small, 1816, Reprinted by AMS Press Inc., 1973), 236

Captain Posey and the rest of Morgan's light corps, numbering nearly 600 men, advanced through the thick wood in two sections.[8] They marched about a mile and a half and emerged onto the edge of an abandoned farm. The clearing was dotted with trees and stumps. Two small buildings, described as cabins by many eyewitnesses, sat on a rise of ground about 300 yards away. The opposite wood line was only 150 yards beyond the cabins.

Morgan's corps arrived at the clearing just as an enemy advance party attacked the American picquet guard posted in the cabins. Samuel Armstrong, a member of Major Dearborn's light infantry, described the encounter:

> [at] *about 12 Oclock we were Alarm'd by the firing of two or three Musketts from the Enemies Scouts, upon which the Riffle and Light Infantry Battalions were Ordered off to Scour the Woods. We forwarded down to our Picquet Guard where we had no sooner got Sight of than we saw the Enemy surrounding them.*[9]

British accounts of the engagement contend that the Americans, probably just the picquet guard, were driven from Freeman's Farm. The Earl of Harrington, an aide to General Burgoyne, claimed that,

---

[8] Wilkinson, Appendix E and
Joseph Lee Boyle, "From Saratoga to Valley Forge: The Diary of Lt. Samuel Armstrong," *The Pennsylvania Magazine of History and Biography*, Vol. 121 No. 3 (July 1997), 245
(Henceforth referred to as Lieutenant Armstrong's Diary)
[9] Lieutenant Armstrong's Diary, 245

The [British] *advance party...fell in with a considerable body of the rebels, posted in a house and behind fences, which they attacked, and after a great deal of fire, the detachment nearly drove in the body of rebels.* [10]

As the British skirmishers pushed past the cabins and approached the southern wood line, they collided with the bulk of Morgan's light corps. British Ensign Thomas Anburey described what happened:

the [British] *advanced party...nearly drove in the body of the Americans, but the woods being filled with men, much annoyed the pickets....* [11]

The British skirmishers, outnumbered and outgunned, fell back under a deadly barrage of fire. British Lieutenant William Digby commented on the impact of Morgan's fire:

A little after 12 our advanced picquets came up with Colonel Morgan and engaged, but from the great superiority of fire received from him – his numbers being much greater – they were obliged to fall back, every officer being either killed or wounded except one. [12]

The lead elements of Morgan's corps pursued the enemy across the field and into the woods beyond. The pursuit came to an abrupt end, however, when the Americans discovered

---

[10] Earl of Harrington in, John Burgoyne, *A State of the Expedition from Canada,* (New York Times & Arno Press, 1969), 68
Note: This account is supported by the observation of American Lieutenant Colonel James Wilkinson, who saw British bodies lying around the cabins after the initial engagement, but prior to the resumption of battle.
[11] Anburey, 172
[12] Digby Journal, 272

British reinforcements in their front. These soldiers, eager to fire on the Americans, did so without orders and before all of their comrades from the advance party had cleared their front.[13] The result was more loss for the battered British skirmishers and an end to the American pursuit.

Morgan's corps, which was already disorganized by the charge, disintegrated in retreat. Men ran in all directions to escape the enemy. The sudden emergence of two British companies, and a cannon from General Fraser's column on the American's left flank, added urgency to their flight.[14]

Appalled by the turn of events, Colonel Morgan worked hard to reorganize his shattered corps. He used an uncommon military tool to do so, a turkey whistle. Colonel Wilkinson, who appeared on the scene soon after the fight, described an encounter with Colonel Morgan and the whistle:

> *my ears were saluted by an uncommon noise, which I approached, and perceived Colonel Morgan attended by two men only, who with a turkey call was collecting his dispersed troops. The moment I came up to him, he burst into tears, and exclaimed, 'I am ruined, by G—d! Major Morris ran on so rapidly with the front, that they were beaten before I could get up with the rear, and my men are scattered God knows where.' I remarked to the Colonel that he had a long day before him to retrieve an inauspicious beginning, and informed him where I had seen his field officers, which appeared to cheer him, and we parted.* [15]

---

[13] Horatio Rogers ed. *Hadden's Journal and Orderly Book: A Journal Kept in Canada and Upon Burgoyne's Campaign in 1776 and 1777*, (Boston: Gregg Press, 1972), 163
(Henceforth referred to as Hadden Journal)
[14] Anburey, 172
[15] Wilkinson, 238

One of the field officers Colonel Wilkinson met prior to Morgan was Major Joseph Morris. Morris led the charge against the fleeing British pickets and provided Wilkinson with a detailed account of the engagement:

> *from him* [Major Morris] *I learnt that the corps was advancing by files in two lines, when they unexpectedly fell upon a picket of the enemy, which they almost instantly forced, and pursuing the fugitives, their front had as unexpectedly fallen in with the British line; that several officers and men had been made prisoners, and that to save himself, he had been obliged to push his horse through the ranks of the enemy, and escaped by a circuitous route.* [16]

Wilkinson also encountered Lieutenant Colonel Richard Butler, the rifle corps' second in command. He confirmed Morris's account:

> *I* [Wilkinson] *crossed the angle of the field, leapt the fence, and just before me on a ridge discovered Lieutenant-colonel Butler with three men, all tree'd; from him I learnt that they had 'caught a Scotch prize,' that having forced the picket, they had closed with the British line, had been instantly routed, and from the suddenness of the shock and the nature of the ground, were broken and scattered in all directions.* [17]

Major Dearborn was a bit less descriptive of the incident in his journal:

---

[16] Ibid., 237
[17] Ibid.

hereing this morning that the Enimy ware advancing,
the Rifle and Light Infantry Corps turned out to meet
the Enimy & about 2 miles from our Camp we fell in
with their advanced Guard & attacked them about 12
O Clock, after fighting about half an hour Being over
Powerd with Numbers we ware Obliged to Retire to
A height, about 50 rods...[800 feet].[18]

It was probably near this hill that Colonel Wilkinson observed Major Dearborn *"with great animation and not a little warmth...forming thirty or forty of his infantry."*[19] Dearborn's efforts to reform his unit were successful, and they joined American reinforcements on the left of the American line.

Thanks to an hour long pause in the conflict, Colonel Morgan was also able to reform his riflemen. They formed in the woods on the extreme right of the American line.[20] A marshy ravine protected their right flank. To their left, fresh American troops from the brigades of General Poor and Learned extended the line westward.

The battle resumed around mid afternoon, when General Hamilton's center column emerged from the far woods and advanced upon the Americans. They concentrated on the hill and ridge upon which the Freeman house stood. Lieutenant James Hadden, a British artillery officer, described the engagement:

The Enemy being in possession of the wood almost
immediately attacked the Corps which took post
beyond two log Huts on Freemans Farm...I was

---

[18] Lloyd A. Brown & Howard H. Peckman, ed., *Revolutionary War Journals of Henry Dearborn: 1775-1783*, (Freeport, NY: Books for Libraries Press, 1939), 105-106
(Henceforth referred to as Dearborn Journal)
[19] Wilkinson, 237
[20] Hadden Journal, 164

advanced with two Guns to the left of the 62nd Regt and ye two left companies being formed en potence [refused or bent to protect the flank] *I took post in the Angle...In this situation we sustained a heavy tho intermitting fire from near three hours....*[21]

The American fire, enhanced by the accuracy of the riflemen, was especially hard on the enemy's artillerymen. Lieutenant Hadden lost 19 out of 22 men and all of his horses. The 62nd regiment lost nearly half of its men. [22]

Hadden's position was not the only hot spot, however. The battle raged all along the line. British Lieutenant William Digby noted that he had never seen anything like it:

such an explosion of fire I never had any idea of before, and the heavy artillery joining in concert like great peals of thunder, assisted by the echoes of the woods, almost deafened us with the noise. [23]

British corporal Roger Lamb gave a similar account:

the conflict was dreadful; for four hours a constant blaze of fire was kept up, and both armies seemed to be determined on death or victory...Men, and particularly officers, dropped every moment on each side. Several of the Americans placed themselves in high trees, and as often as they could distinguish a British officer's uniform, took him off by deliberately aiming at his person.[24]

---

[21] Ibid., 165
[22] Ibid.
[23] Digby Journal, 237
[24] Roger Lamb, *An Original and Authentic Journal of Occurrences During the Late American War from Its Commencement to 1783*, (Dublin: Wilkinson & Courtney, 1809), 159
Reprinted by Arno Press, 1968

The impact of American markmenship was also noted by Colonel James Wilkinson, who observed that it repeatedly drove the British from the Freeman house hill:

> *the fire of our marksmen from this wood was too deadly to be withstood by the enemy in line, and when they gave way and broke, our men rushing from their cover, pursued them to the eminence, where having their flanks protected, they [the enemy] rallied and charging in turn drove us back into the wood, from whence a dreadful fire would again force them to fall back; and in this manner did the battle fluctuate, like waves of a stormy sea, with alternate advantage for four hours without one moment's intermission. The British artillery fell into our possession at every charge, but we could neither turn the pieces upon the enemy, nor bring them off...The slaughter of this brigade of artillerists was remarkable, the captain and thirty-six men being killed or wounded out of forty-eight.*[25]

Even General Burgoyne acknowledged the impact of the riflemen:

> *The enemy had with their army great numbers of marksmen, armed with rifle-barrel pieces; these during an engagement, hovered upon the flanks in small detachments, and were very expert in securing themselves, and in shifting their ground. In this action many placed themselves in high trees in the rear of their own line, and there was seldom a minute's interval of smoke, in any part of our line without officers being taken off by single shot. It will naturally be supposed, that the Indians would be of*

---

[25] Wilkinson, 241

great use against this mode of fighting. The example of those that remained after the great desertion proved the contrary, for not a man of them was to be brought within the sound of a rifle shot. [26]

As sunset approached, the British were in serious trouble. The 62nd regiment was shattered and the other regiments were barely holding on. Suddenly, the sound of drums came from the woods beyond the American right flank. German reinforcements, under General Riedesel, emerged from the forest and onto the field to relieve the British. They slammed into the right flank of the startled Americans. A German artillery officer, Captain Pausch, recalled that,

I had shells brought up and placed by the side of the cannon and as soon as I got the range, I fired twelve or fourteen shots in quick succession into the foe who were within good pistol shot distance. [27]

The arrival of the Germans revived British spirits, and they rallied one more time. Captain Pausch noted that,

The firing from muskets was at once renewed, and assumed lively proportions, particularly the platoon fire from the left wing of Riedesel. Presently, the enemy's fire, though very lively at one time, suddenly ceased. I advanced about sixty paces sending a few shells after the flying enemy, and firing from twelve to fifteen shots more into the woods into which they had retreated. Everything then became quiet; and about fifteen minutes afterwards darkness set in. [28]

---

[26] Burgoyne, 39-40

[27] George Pausch, *Journal of Captain Pausch, Chief of the Hanau Artillery During the Burgoyne Campaign,* Translated by William L. Stone, (Albany, NY: Joel Munsell's Sons, 1886), 137-138

[28] Ibid., 138

One of the most intense battles of the Revolutionary War was over, and the carnage was appalling. The field was littered with dead and wounded men who remained unattended all night. Lieutenant Digby described the scene:

During the night we remained in our ranks, and tho we heard the groans of our wounded and dying at a small distance, yet could not assist them till morning, not knowing the position of the enemy, and expecting the action would be renewed at day break. Sleep was a stranger to us, but we were all in good spirits and ready to obey with cheerfulness and orders the general might issue before morning dawned.
20th. At day break we sent out parties to bring in our wounded, and lit fires as we were almost froze with cold, and our wounded who lived till the morning must have severely felt it. [29]

British ensign Thomas Anburey had the misfortune to command a burial party in the morning:

The day after our late engagement, I had as unpleasant a duty as can fall to the lot of an officer, the command of the party sent out to bury the dead and bring in the wounded...They [the wounded] had remained out all night, and from the loss of blood and want of nourishment, were upon the point of expiring with faintness; some of them begged they might lie and die, others again were insensible, some upon the least movement were put in the most horrid tortures, and all had near a mile to be conveyed to the hospitals; others at their last gasp, who for want of our timely assistance must have inevitably expired. These poor creatures, perishing with cold and

---

[29] Digby, 274

weltering in their blood, displayed such a scene, it must be a heart of adamant that could not be affected at it....[30]

Although the British kept the field, and thus considered themselves the victors, they paid a heavy price, suffering twice as many casualties as the Americans. Some of the British, like Thomas Anburey, questioned the value of the victory:

Notwithstanding the glory of the day remains on our side, I am fearful the real advantage resulting from this hard fought battle will rest on that of the Americans, our army being so weakened by this engagement as not to be of sufficient strength to venture forth and improve the victory, which may, in the end, put a stop to our intended expedition; the only apparent benefit gained is that we keep possession of the ground where the engagement began.[31]

General Burgoyne, in a letter to Lord George Germain, reached a similar conclusion about the victory:

It was soon found that no fruits, honour excepted, were attained by the preceding victory, the enemy working with redoubled ardour to strengthen their left, their right was already unattackable.[32]

---

[30] Anburey, 176

[31] Ibid., 175

[32] "Burgoyne to Germaine, 10 October, 1777", in *A State of the Expedition,* Appendix, 88

Despite their retreat from the field, the attitude in the American camp was far from defeatist. In fact, most American accounts bragged about punishing the enemy and attributed the retreat merely to darkness. Major Dearborn's observation was typical:

> *the Enimy Brought almost their whole force against us, together with 8 pieces of Artilery. But we who had Something more at Stake than fighting for six Pence Pr Day kept our ground til Night, Closed the scene, & then Both Parties Retire'd.* [33]

Captain Posey proudly wrote years later that, "*The battle of this day broke the heart of Burgoyne's army*...[and] *Morgans regiment did great execution.*"[34]

Major Dearborn was also proud, recording in his journal that,

> *on this Day has Been fought one of the Greatest Battles that Ever was fought in America, & I Trust we have Convinced the British Butchers that the Cowardly yankees Can & when there is a Call for it, will, fight.* [35]

This change of attitude did indeed occur among the British. Many, including Ensign Anburey, commented on the conduct of the Americans:

> *The courage and obstinacy with which the Americans fought were the astonishment of everyone, and we now become fully convinced they are not that contemptible enemy we had hitherto imagined them,*

---

[33] Dearborn Journal, 106
[34] Posey Biography
[35] Dearborn Journal, 106-107

incapable of standing a regular engagement, and that they would only fight behind strong and powerful works.[36]

Captain Posey and his men were proud of their participation in the battle. Along with the rest of Morgan's light corps, they fought from beginning to end. Despite their heavy involvement, the riflemen suffered only sixteen casualties, seven killed and nine wounded. [37] The longer range of rifles, which allowed Morgan's men to fire at the enemy from beyond musket distance, contributed to the low casualties. In contrast, Major Dearborn's light infantry battalion, armed with smoothbore muskets, had the highest number of unit deaths, with eighteen. Twenty-two others were wounded. [38] An official count of American casualties listed 321 in all, with 65 killed, 218 wounded, and 38 missing. [39]

Although the Americans believed they had dealt the enemy a significant blow, they realized that Burgoyne's army was still very dangerous. In fact, on September 20th, they braced themselves for another British attack. Fortunately for the Americans, who were low on ammunition, it never materialized.

General Burgoyne had actually planned to attack the Americans that day, but he canceled the attack at the last second to rest his troops. The next day, Burgoyne received a message from General Henry Clinton that significantly affected his plans. General Clintion informed Burgoyne that he was leading a detachment northward from New York to attack the American posts in the New York Highlands and draw some of General's Gates' troops away from Bemis Heights. Although Clinton's force was too small to fight its

---

[36] Anburey, 175
[37] Wilkinson, Appendix D
[38] Ibid.
[39] Ibid.

way to General Burgoyne, Clinton hoped his march north would give General Burgoyne a better chance to break through to Albany.

General Burgoyne decided to fortify his current position and wait for Clinton's advance to have the desired effect on the American army at Bemis Heights. Unfortunately for Burgoyne, Clinton's advance drew few of the enemy away. In fact, during the seventeen day standoff, the American army, bolstered by thousands of militia troops, swelled to well over 10,000 men. [40]

The ever cautious General Gates kept most of his men within the fortified lines. Time was on his side. Every day saw the enemy's provisions dwindle, and their situation grow more desperate. Colonel Morgan's light corps added to Burgoyne's discomfort by constantly harassing his lines and foraging parties. General Burgoyne acknowledged the inability of his troops to gather forage in a letter after the battle:

From the 20th of September to the 7th of October, the armies were so near, that not a single night passed without firing, and sometimes concerted attacks upon our advanced picquets; no foraging party could be made without great detachments to cover it; it was the plan of the enemy to harass the army by constant alarms, and their superiority of numbers enabled them to attempt it without fatigue to themselves. [41]

Major Henry Dearborn recalled in his memoirs that in the weeks following the first battle,

---

[40] Wilkinson, "A General Return of the Army of the United States, commanded by the Hon. Major-General Horatio Gates, 4 Oct. 1777" Appendix E
[41] Burgoyne, 168

Our light troops were constantly employed at reconnoitering the Enemy and had some skirmishing.... [42]

The value of this corps, especially the riflemen, was highlighted in an exchange of letters between General Washington and General Gates. On September 24th, General Washington congratulated Gates on his success at Freeman's Farm. He then requested the return of Morgan's riflemen to the main army:

> *This Army has not been able to oppose General Howe's with the success that was wished, and needs a Reinforcement. I therefore request, if you have been so fortunate, as to Oblige General Burgoyne to retreat to Tyconderoga—or If you have not and circumstances will admit, that you will Order Colo. Morgan to Join me again with his Corps. I sent him up when I thought you materially wanted him, and if his services can be dispensed with now, you will direct his return immediately. [43]*

The fact that Washington only requested the Rifle Corps's return is a testament of his high regard for the unit. General Gates' response was equally telling of his own esteem and reliance on the riflemen:

> *Since the Action of the 19th Instant, the Enemy have kept the Ground they Occupied the Morning of that Day, And fortified their Camp. The Advanced*

---

[42] Henry Dearborn, "A Narrative of the Saratoga Campaign – Major General Henry Dearborn, 1815, *The Bulletin of the Fort Ticonderoga Museum, Vol. 1 no. 5* (January, 1929), 7
(Henceforth referred to as Dearborn's Memoir)
[43] "General Washington to General Gates, 24 September, 1777", *The Papers of George Washington, Vol. 11,* 310

Centrys of my picquets, are posted within Shot, And Opposite the Enemy's; neither side have given Ground an Inch. In this Situation, Your Excellency would not wish me to part with the Corps the Army of General Burgoyne are most Afraid of. [44]

General Gates added that with British provisions dwindling, it was only a matter of days or weeks before the enemy either risked an attack or withdrew to Ticonderoga. Gates was confident of success, in either case, and informed Washington that he hoped to soon send far more than one regiment as a re-enforcement. [45]

The day after he wrote to Washington, General Gates ordered the light corps, along with 400 additional troops, to reconnoiter the enemy's lines. They circled around to the rear of the British and captured seven prisoners.[46] Major Dearborn reported that,

as we Returned, Night comeing on, together with a heavy Rain, we got Bewildered in the woods & Stayed all night.[47]

While Captain Posey and the rest of Morgan's light corps endured a miserable night in the field, General Burgoyne prepared to act. His supply situation was critical. Burgoyne decided to probe the American position with a large reconnaissance detachment. If the reconnaissance discovered a weakness in the American position, he would follow with an attack the next day. If no weakness was found, then the army would commence a retreat to Fort Ticonderoga.

---

[44] "General Gates to General Washington, 5 October, 1777", *The Papers of George Washington, Vol. 11*, 392
[45] Ibid.
[46] Dearborn Journal, 108
[47] Ibid.

Battle of Bemis Heights

General Burgoyne's reconnaissance force numbered approximately 1,500 men and ten cannon.[48] Although nearly all of the army's units contributed men, the bulk came from the right wing of Burgoyne's line. Two redoubts anchored this position. One was manned by British light infantry under Lieutenant Colonel Balcarress. The other was defended by German grenadiers under Lieutenant Colonel Breymann. Since the march route of the reconnaissance detachment placed it between the Americans and the redoubts, General Burgoyne drew heavily from these fortifications and left only a skeleton force in each.[49]

Burgoyne led his troops out of camp around noon and slowly advanced toward the American left wing. After less than a mile, his skirmishers confronted American picquets and drove them off. Burgoyne halted at the Barber farm and posted his men in a long line facing the Americans. The British right flank, composed of light infantry troops, rested in a clearing at the base of a wooded hill. German troops, supported by artillery, held the center of the line, and the left was defended by British grenadiers and artillery.[50]

General Burgoyne attempted to observe the American line from Barber's farm, but the woods obscured his view. Ironically, as Burgoyne and his staff struggled to peer through the woods, they were observed by an American officer.

When reports of Burgoyne's advance reached American headquarters, General Gates dispatched his aide, Lieutenant Colonel Wilkinson, to investigate:

---

[48] Eric Schnitzer, "Battling for the Saratoga Landscape", *Cultural Landscape Report: Saratoga Battle, Saratoga National Park, Vol. 1* (Boston, MA: Olmsted Center for Landscape Preservation), 44
[49] Ibid.
[50] Luzader, 52

I perceived about half a mile from the line of our encampment, several columns of the enemy, 60 or 70 rods from me, entering a wheat field which had not been cut, and was separated from me by a small rivulet...After entering the field, they displayed, formed the line, and sat down in double ranks with their arms between their legs. Foragers then proceeded to cut the wheat or standing straw, and I soon after observed several officers, mounted on the top of a cabin, from whence their glasses they were endeavoring to reconnoitre our left, which was concealed from their view by intervening woods. [51]

Wilkinson reported his findings to General Gates, who then sent Wilkinson to Colonel Morgan with instructions to, *"begin the game."* [52] Wilkinson recalled that,

I waited on the Colonel, whose corps was formed in front of our centre, and delivered the order; he knew the ground, and inquired the position of the enemy: they were formed across a newly cultivated field, their grenadiers with several pieces on the left, bordering on a wood and a small ravine...their light infantry on the right, covered by a worm fence at the foot of the hill...thickly covered with wood; their centre composed of British and German battalions. Colonel Morgan, with his usual sagacity, proposed to make a circuit with his corps by our left, and under cover of the wood to gain the height on the right of the enemy, and from thence commence his attack, so soon as our fire should be opened against their left. [53]

---

[51] Wilkinson, 267
[52] Ibid., 268
[53] Ibid.

General Gates approved Morgan's proposal and ordered Poor's brigade to attack Burgoyne's left flank. General Learned's brigade followed, with instructions to strike the center of the enemy line.

As Colonel Morgan's men hurried to gain possession of the wooded hill overlooking Burgoyne's right flank, fighting erupted on the left. The intensity of the engagement caused some in Morgan's corps to worry that the Americans were losing ground. Major Dearborn recalled that,

> *our light troops moved on with a quick step in the course directed, and after ascending the woody hill to a small field about 500 yards to the right of the Enemies main line, we discovered a body of British light Infantry handsomely posted on a ridge 150 yards from the edge of the wood where we then were. At this time the fire of the two main armies was unusually heavy and we were apprehensive from the fire that our line was giving way.* [54]

Colonel Morgan rushed his men towards the enemy flank. Captain Posey described what happened:

> *They* [the enemy] *had repulsed* [General] *Arnold twice before Morgan made his attack, which was on the right wing of* [the] *enemy – the* [rifle] *regiment had march'd under cover of a thick wood, and a ridge, which ridge the enemy were about to take possession of as Morgan gained the summit of it, the enemy being within good rifle shot, the regiment poured in a well directed fire which brought almost every officer on horseback to the ground.* [55]

---

[54] Dearborn Memoir, 7
[55] Posey Biography

Lieutenant Colonel Richard Butler also noted the impact of the riflemen in the attack:

> *I had the Honour to lead the Corps of Riflemen Against their Right wing Under Morgan, Who Commanded in Center of the Whole, our light troops About 1000, & Can say without Ostenation that we saved the day by our timely & vigourous Attack (I believe the Indian Hoop helped A little) as we broke the Right Wing of the Enemy took two 12 Pounders & one six and turned them on them.* [56]

Lieutenant Colonel Wilkinson's account of the engagement suggests that the riflemen and light infantry operated separately:

> *True to his purpose, Morgan at this critical moment poured down like a torrent from the hill, and attacked the right of the enemy in front and flank. Dearborn at the moment, when the enemy's light infantry were attempting to change front, [to face the riflemen] pressed forward with ardour and delivered a close fire; then lept the fence, shouted, charged and gallantly forced them in disorder.* [57]

Interestingly, Major Dearborn's account states that the light infantry charged the enemy without firing a shot:

> *We...determined to make a dash on this body of the Enemy* [light infantry] *and endeavour to force our way on the rear of the Enemies main body. We accordingly agreed to jump over the fence, raise a*

---

[56] Lt. Col. Richard Butler to Col. James Wilson, 22 January, 1778
   Gratz Collection, Case 4, Box 11, Historical Society of Pennsylvania
[57] Wilkinson, 268

shout and run upon the Enemy without firing. We acted accordingly and the Enemy gave way and ran in disorder without firing a shot.[58]

Stunned by the sudden attack of Morgan's light corps, the British right flank collapsed. Things were no better for Burgoyne on his left flank, where his grenadiers were decimated by General Poor's men.

Despite the collapse of his flanks, Burgoyne's center held firm. Furthermore, the commander of the British right flank, General Fraser, worked hard to restore the line. His efforts abruptly ended, however, when one of Morgan's riflemen shot him from his horse. Fraser died the next day.

The pressure on the center of Burgoyne's line soon proved too great, and it joined the rest of the detachment in retreat. Eight British cannon and scores of men were abandoned on the field. Lt. Colonel Wilkinson described the carnage:

The ground which had been occupied by the British grenadiers presented a scene of complicated horror and exultation. In the square space of twelve or fifteen yards lay eighteen grenadiers in the agonies of death, and three officers propped up against stumps of trees, two of them mortally wounded, bleeding, and almost speechless.[59]

Most of Burgoyne's detachment, including 300 German grenadiers who were drawn from Breymann's redoubt, retreated to the Balcarres redoubt. This bolstered the defenders there, but left Breymann's redoubt (on the extreme right of the British line) undermanned and vulnerable. Two fortified cabins between the redoubts were also weakly manned, due to the failure of soldiers to return to them.

---

[58] Dearborn Memoir, 7
[59] Wilkinson, 270

Initially, these vulnerable positions were not a problem for the British, because the Americans concentrated their attack on the Balcarres redoubt. British corporal, Roger Lamb, recalled that,

> *General Arnold with a brigade of continental troops, pushed rapidly forward, for that part of the camp possessed by lord Balcarres, at the head of the British light infantry, and some of the line; here they were received by a heavy and well directed fire which moved down their ranks, and compelled them to retreat in disorder.* [60]

Lieutenant Colonel Wilkinson also noted the intensity of the fight at the Balcarres redoubt:

> *the roar of cannon and small arms at this juncture was sublime, between the enemy, behind their works and our troops entirely exposed, or partially sheltered by trees, stumps, or hollows, at various distances not exceeding 120 yards.* [61]

Although the attack on the Balcarres redoubt was repulsed, the Americans maintained a heavy fire on the fort. A few hundred yards away, Colonel Morgan's corps prepared to storm the Breymann redoubt and win the day.

Morgan's men had advanced very close to the redoubt and used a steep hill in their front to protect them from enemy fire.[62] Other American units formed to the right of the light corps and engaged the enemy. Lieutenant Colonel Wilkinson described the scene:

---

[60] Lamb, 164
[61] Wilkinson, 271
[62] Schnitzer, 50

61

The Germans were encamped immediately behind the rail breast-work, and the ground in front of it declined in a very gentle slope for about 120 yards, when it sunk abruptly; our troops had formed a line under this declivity, and covered breast high were warmly engaged with the Germans. [63]

The Americans were soon reinforced by General Learned's brigade. Wilkinson informed General Learned of a weak spot in the enemy line, two sparsely manned fortified cabins, and recommended that the brigade attack there:

I had particularly examined the ground between the left of the Germans and the light infantry, occupied by the provincialists, from whence I had observed a slack fire; I therefore recommended to General Learned to incline to his right, and attack at that point: he did so with great gallantry; the provincialists abandoned their position and fled; the German flank was by this means uncovered. [64]

As Learned's brigade advanced, they were joined by General Benedict Arnold, who, without orders, assumed command of the attack. Colonel Wilkinson recalled that Arnold,

dashed to the left through the fire of the two lines and escaped unhurt; he then turned the right of the enemy, as I was informed by that most excellent officer, Colonel Butler, and collecting 15 or 20 riflemen threw himself with this party into the rear of the enemy, just as they gave way, where his leg was broke, and his horse killed under him. [65]

---

[63] Wilkinson, 272
[64] Ibid.
[65] Ibid., 272

Lieutenant Colonel Richard Butler, of the rifle corps, gave a similar account of the engagement:

> *Genl. Arnold was the first of Entered, one Major Morris with about 12 of the Rifle men followed him on the Rear of their Right Flank while I led up the rest of the Riflemen in front. I was the 3rd officer in* [the redoubt]. [66]

Major Dearborn's light infantry also participated in the assault of the redoubt and described it in his memoirs:

> *The assault was commenced by the advance of Arnold with about 200 men through a cops of wood which covered the Enemies right, the appearance of Arnold on the right was the signal for us to advance and assault the front. The whole was executed in the most spirited and prompted manner and as soon as the Enemy had given us one fire, he fell back from his work to his line of tents, and as we entered he gave way and retreated in confusion.* [67]

As Morgan's light corps swarmed over the walls and through the sally port and embrasures, General Arnold struck the German rear.

Whether by design or chance, the assault on Breymann's redoubt was masterfully executed, and the Germans were quickly overwhelmed. General Burgoyne's line was breeched and only nightfall saved the British from further disaster.

Once again, the American army had punished the enemy, inflicting far more casualties than they had suffered. This decisive victory left General Burgoyne with only one choice,

---

[66] Lt. Col. Richard Butler to Col. James Wilson, 22 January, 1778
[67] Dearborn Memoir, 8

retreat. His march to Albany was over. It remained to be seen whether his retreat to Fort Ticonderoga would succeed.

Retreat and Surrender

Under cover of darkness, General Burgoyne withdrew his army across the Great Ravine and established a new position on a hill overlooking the Hudson River. The position was called the Great Redoubt, and its location allowed Burgoyne to consolidate his troops and protect the river transports and hospital.

When the Americans realized that Burgoyne had withdrawn across the ravine, they took possession of the old lines and commenced a steady, but ineffectual, bombardment. General Gates sent Morgan's light corps forward to reconnoiter the enemy's rear and harass them. Major Dearborn participated in this reconnaissance:

this morning [Oct. 8] *the Rifle men & Light Infantry & several other Regiments march'd in the Rear of the Enimy Expecting they ware Retreeting But found they ware Not. there has Been scurmishing all Day...a Large Number of the Enimy Deserted to us to Day.*[68]

General Burgoyne realized that retreat or surrender were the only options left for his army. The former would be tremendously difficult, but the latter was still unthinkable. Thus, on the evening of October 8th, Burgoyne began a retreat northward. Over 400 men, too injured or sick to transport, were left to the care of the Americans. The rest of Burgoyne's army slowly trudged towards Saratoga.

After only a few miles, they halted to rest and wait for the boats to catch up. A heavy rain pelted the men all day, and when they resumed their march, the road turned to mud. They

---

[68] Dearborn Journal, 109

arrived at the heights of Saratoga after dark and collapsed on the ground in exhaustion. Lieutenant Digby described the scene:

> *we remained all night under constant, heavy rain without fires or any kind of shelter to guard us from the inclemency of the weather. It was impossible to sleep, even had we an inclination to do so from the cold and rain....*[69]

Ensign Anburey gave an equally distressing account of the army's first night in Saratoga:

> *the army...arrived at Saratoga, in such a state of fatigue that the men had not strength or inclination to cut wood and make fires, but rather sought sleep in their wet clothes and on the wet ground.*[70]

Despite Burgoyne's slow retreat, the Americans struggled to keep pace. The rain turned the road into a quagmire of mud and the size of the American army, over 12,000 strong, complicated logistics. Fortunately for the Americans, Burgoyne's retreat ceased at Saratoga.

Over the next few days, as General Burgoyne grappled with his situation, the American riflemen and light infantry constantly harassed them. A steady artillery bombardment added to their discomfort. By October 14th, General Burgoyne and his army had had enough. With his officer's consent, Burgoyne asked for terms of surrender. General Gates was generous in his demands, and on October 17th, General Burgoyne formally surrendered his army.

---

[69] Digby, 300
[70] Anburey, 190

The most decisive battle of the Revolutionary War to date was over, and riflemen from the 7th Virginia regiment, under Captain Thomas Posey, played a crucial role in the victory.

Chapter Four

Brandywine to Whitemarsh

While Captain Posey and his riflemen celebrated the momentous victory at Saratoga, the rest of the 7th Virginia, along with General Washington's army, sat outside enemy held Philadelphia. Washington's troops had struggled for weeks to defend the city, losing two hard fought battles in the process. The bulk of the American army, including General William Woodford's brigade to which the 7th Virginia belonged, fought admirably in these engagements. Unfortunately, bad intelligence, weather, and luck undermined their efforts.

The Battle of Brandywine

Nearly a week before the first battle of Saratoga, thousands of men under General William Howe and General George Washington confronted each other near a small creek in Pennsylvania. Weeks of maneuvering brought the two armies to Brandywine Creek, 25 miles southwest of Philadelphia.

General Howe, in command of nearly 15,000 men, attempted to reach the creek before Washington's army, which was roughly equal in size, could oppose its crossing.[1] Washington arrived first, however, and took up a strong position in the hills overlooking the east bank of the creek. Although he held the main crossing point at Chadd's Ford, Washington's defense of the Brandywine was complicated by the existence of a number of fords to the north. As a result, he was forced to spread his army along a five mile front.

---

[1] Samuel Smith, *The Battle of Brandywine*, (Monmouth Beach, NJ: Philip Freneau Press, 1976), 6

Most of the 7th Virginia, still commanded by Colonel Alexander McClanahan, was posted a few miles north of Chadd's Ford with Woodford's brigade. They anxiously waited for General Howe to act. A portion of the regiment was much closer to the enemy, however. They were part of the American advanced guard under General William Maxwell. This special unit of light infantry, drawn from all of the brigades, was formed in late August to replace Colonel Morgan's rifle corps. Maxwell's men had already engaged General Howe's troops in a sharp skirmish a week earlier near Cooches Bridge, Delaware. Now they were posted across the Brandywine along the likely march route of Howe's army.

Maxwell's 800 man detachment was not expected to stop the British army, but rather to harass and delay its advance. Like their comrades across the creek, they anxiously awaited General Howe's next move. It came on the morning of September 11th.

Howe's plan was simple. General Knyphausen, with nearly 7,000 men, would march directly towards the Americans at Chadd's Ford to mislead General Washington into thinking that the main attack was there. While the Americans focused on this movement, General Cornwallis, with over 8,000 men, accompanied by General Howe, would cross the Brandywine north of the American line to strike Washington's right flank. [2] If all went as planned, the American army would be crushed between the two columns.

Howe's columns began their march at daybreak. Less than two miles into the march, General Knyphausen's advanced guard engaged a party of Maxwell's men. The American detachment, commanded by Captain Charles Porterfield of the 11th Virginia, surprised them with a deadly volley near the Kennett Meeting House. A few of Knyphausen's men fell, but the rest pressed on and pursued Porterfield to the next American position. Maxwell's men waged a fighting retreat

---

[2] Smith, 9

for more than three hours, using trees, fences, and stone walls for cover. The force of the British attack was too great to stop, however, and by 10:30 a.m., Maxwell's detachment was pushed across the Brandywine. [3]

The rest of the American army, including the 7th Virginia listened to the approaching battle and braced for combat. They expected the enemy to cross the creek at any moment. Instead, a long lull ensued. When the quiet extended into the afternoon, General Washington became suspicious. Conflicting reports of enemy troop movements towards his right flank paralyzed him with indecision.

Initially, when he was told that General Howe had divided his army, Washington saw an opportunity to attack his weaker foe across the Brandywine. However, new reports contradicted the original one and caused Washington to hesitate. By the time he determined that General Howe had indeed divided his army, the opportunity to attack was lost, and Washington had to scramble to protect his right flank. He ordered Generals Sullivan, Stirling, and Stephen to reposition their divisions to oppose Howe's attack. The 7th Virginia, along with the rest of Woodford's brigade and Stephen's division, raced eastward to gain the hills overlooking the Birmingham Meeting House. The other divisions followed and formed on the left of Stephen's division. General Woodford's brigade held the right flank of the American line. They were deployed on a hill about 300 yards southwest of the Meeting House.

Woodford placed his most experienced regiment, Colonel Thomas Marshall's 3rd Virginia, in advance and to the right of his brigade to cover his exposed right flank. Marshall's 170 men passed the Birmingham Meeting House and took post in

---

[3] John F. Reed, *Campaign to Valley Forge: July 1, 1777 – December 19, 1777* (Pioneer Press, 1980), 120

an orchard. They were ordered to, *"hold the wood as long as it was tenable."* [4]

About a mile to the north, General Howe's men prepared to attack. Howe's advance guard approached the 3rd Virginia around 3:30 p.m. Colonel Marshall's men, assisted by General Woodford's cannon, delivered such a hot fire that the enemy halted and took shelter behind a fence. Captain Johann Ewald, commander of the British advance guard, described the encounter:

> *About half past three I caught sight of some infantry and horsemen behind a village on a hill in the distance. I drew up at once and deployed...I reached the first houses of the village with the flankers of the jagers, and Lt. Hagen followed me with the horsemen. But unfortunately for us, the time this took favored the enemy and I received extremely heavy small-arms fire from the gardens and houses, through which, however, only two jagers were wounded. Everyone ran back, and I formed them again behind the fences or walls at a distance of two hundred paces from the village....* [5]

Ewald remained at the fence until the main line of General Howe's troops reached him, at which point he and his men resumed their advance. The British pushed the 3rd Virginia out of the orchard and to the Meeting House grounds, where the Virginians used a stone wall for cover. Marshall's men

---

[4] Brigadier General George Weedon's Correspondence Account of the Battle of Brandywine, 11 September, 1777. The original manuscript is in the collections of the Chicago Historical Society, Transcribed by Bob McDonald, 2001

[5] Captain Johann Ewald, *Diary of the American War: A Hessian Journal*, translated & edited by Joseph Tustin (New Haven: Yale Univ. Press, 1979), 84-85

fought so hard that the enemy veered around their flanks, rather than confront them directly at the wall.[6]

Despite their brave stand, the Virginians could not hold their position indefinitely. With enemy troops passing both flanks, and nearly a quarter of their men killed or wounded, the 3rd Virginia had no choice but to retreat. Their struggle lasted less than an hour, but earned them respect for years to come.

General George Weedon observed that Colonel Marshall,

> *received the Enemy with a Firmness which will do Honor to him & his little Corps, as long as the 11th of Sepr. is remembered. He continued there ¾ of one Hour, & must have done amazing execution.* "[7]

General Light Horse Harry Lee concurred. Lee wrote in his memoirs that the 3rd Virginia,

> *bravely sustained itself against superior numbers, never yielding one inch of ground and expending thirty rounds a man, in forty-five minutes.* [8]

The battle now shifted to the hill and ridge southwest of the Birmingham Meetinghouse. Three American divisions held the hill, but one, General Sullivan's, stayed only briefly. It was in the process of coming onto line and linking with General Stirling's division, on their right, when the main British line attacked. General Sullivan explained what happened in a letter to Congress:

---

[6] Smith, 18
[7] Weedon Correspondence
[8] Henry Lee, *The Revolutionary War Memoirs of General Henry Lee*, (New York: Da Capo Press, 1998, Originally Published in 1812), 89-90

71

While my Division was marching out & before it was possible for them to form to advantage, the Enemy pressed on with Rapidity & attacked them which threw them into Some kind of Confusion. [9]

General Sullivan was in charge of the entire right wing of the army, so he left it to his division officers to rally and reform the division, a task they failed to do.

Although the left flank of the American line was in disarray, the rest of the line, supported by heavy artillery fire, held firm.[10] An unidentified British officer described the effect of the American fire:

There was a most infernal Fire of cannon & musketry, most incessant shouting – incline to the right! incline to the left! halt ! charge etc. The balls ploughing up the ground. The Trees cracking over our heads. The branches riven by the artillery – The leaves falling as in autumn by the grapeshot.[11]

Despite the intense fire, the British pushed forward to the base of the hill:

The Enemy soon began to bend their principal force against the Hill," wrote General Sullivan to Congress, *"& the fire was close & heavy for a Long time & soon became General...five times did the*

---

[9] "Before and After the Battle of Brandywine: Extracts from the Journal of Sergeant Thomas Sullivan of H.M. Forty-Ninth Regiment of Foot", 3 September, 1777 in *The Pennsylvania Magazine of History and Biography, Vol. 31*, (Philadelphia: Historical Society of Pennsylvania, 1907), 464

[10] Smith, 18

[11] "The Actions at Brandywine and Paoli, Described by a British Officer", *The Pennsylvania Magazine of History and Biography, Vol. 24*, (Philadelphia: Historical Society of Pennsylvania, 1905), 368

Enemy drive our Troops from the Hill & as often was it Regained & the Summit often Disputed almost muzzle to muzzle...The General fire of the Line Lasted an hour & forty minutes Fifty one minutes of which the Hill was disputed almost Muzzle to Muzzle in such a manner that General Conway who has seen much Service Says he never Say so close & Severe a fire — on the Right where General Stephen was it was Long & Severe & on the Left Considerable.... [12]

Throughout the fight, the 7th Virginia held firm with Woodford's brigade. The severity of the British attack, however, eventually forced the Americans off the hill. General Charles Scott's brigade, holding the left part of General Stephen's division, was the first to give way.[13] That opened a gap between Woodford's men, on the right, and General Stirling's division. The enemy pushed though the gap and pressed General Stirling's division. Lieutenant Ebenezer Elmer, a Surgeon's Mate in the 3rd New Jersey Regiment in Stirling's division, described what happened:

the Battle...proved Excessive severe the Enemy Came on with fury our men stood firing upon them most amazingly, killing almost all before them for near an hour till they got within 6 rod [about 100 feet] of each other, when a Column of the Enemy came upon our right [which] caused [us] to give way [which] soon extended all along [the] line. [14]

---

[12] Sullivan, 464

[13] Smith, 18 and Weedon Correspondence

[14] "The Journal of Ebenezer Elmer," *The Pennsylvania Magazine of History and Biography, Vol. 35* (Philadelphia: Historical Society of Pennsylvania, 1911), 105

The 7th Virginia, and the rest of General Woodford's brigade, was the last American unit to retreat.[15] Their determined stand provided General Sullivan and General Stirling with enough time to rally their men on the next hill in the rear. The Virginians' obstinacy came with a heavy price, however, as they lost their cannon and numerous men, including General Woodford, who was wounded in the hand.[16]

As Woodford's brigade withdrew, they were suddenly attacked on their flank and thrown into confusion. They were saved by the timely arrival of two Virginia brigades under Generals George Weedon and Peter Muhlenberg. These units comprised General Nathaniel Greene's division and rushed four miles in forty-five minutes to cover the collapsing right wing of the American army.[17]

The battle resumed near the village of Dillworth, where Weedon and Muhlenberg's brigades successfully held off the British long enough to allow Washington's army to withdraw. Nightfall put an end to the fighting. Once again, the British scored a victory, chasing the Americans from the field and inflicting twice as many casualties as they endured.[18] Yet, the victory was not complete because Washington's army remained a viable force with plenty of fight still in them.

---

[15] Smith, 19
[16] Smith, 19 and Weedon Correspondence
[17] Weedon Correspondence
[18] Reed, 140

The Battle of Germantown

In the weeks following Brandywine, General Washington struggled to restore the army and protect Philadelphia. Just four days after the battle he signaled his determination to fight on, and his expectation that the army would do likewise:

> *if in time of action, any man who is not wounded whether he has arms or not, turns his back upon the enemy, and attempts to run away, or to retreat before orders are given for it, officers are instantly to put him to death – The man does not deserve to live, who basely flies, breaks his solemn engagements, and betrays his country.* [19]

This policy was not tested until after Philadelphia fell to the British. In late September, General Howe successfully outmaneuvered Washington, so that the British entered the city unopposed. Washington explained what happened to Congress:

> *the Enemy extended themselves up the* [Schuylkill] *river,* [away from Philadelphia] *as if they meant to turn our Right and, countermarching in the night crossed some miles below us; It is probably some the their Parties have entered the City and their whole Army may, if they incline to do it, without our being able to prevent them.* [20]

---

[19] "General Orders, 15 September, 1777", *The Papers of George Washington, Vol. 11*, 233

[20] "General Washington to Thomas Nelson Jr., 27 September, 1777", *The Papers of George Washington, Vol. 11*, 333

Ironically, General Howe's occupation of Philadelphia presented General Washington with an opportunity. Howe needed to open the Delaware River for his supply transports, but two American forts stood in the way. Howe sent a detachment down the river to help capture the forts. Another detachment was posted about five miles above Philadelphia, in the village of Germantown. This force, of 7,000 to 8,000 men, was vulnerable to an American attack, and General Washington seized the opportunity. [21]

Washington's 12,000 man army advanced towards Germantown in four columns on October 4th. [22] The 7th Virginia marched with the rest of Woodford's brigade in one of the center columns. They were still attached to General Stephen's division and were placed in General Nathaniel Greene's column for the attack. General Sullivan commanded the other center column.

General Washington wanted to converge on the enemy's advance guard from four different directions, but coordinating such a movement proved difficult. When General Sullivan, engaged the enemy at sunrise, General Greene was still forty minutes away.[23] Fortunately for the Americans, Sullivan's attack was successful and drove the enemy rearward. General Washington, who accompanied Sullivan's column, described the attack in a letter to Congress:

> *Genl Sullivans advanced party...attacked their picket at Mount Ariy...about Sun rise...which presently gave way, and his Main body* [Sullivan's]...*soon engaged the* [enemy] *Light Infantry and Other Troops encamped near the picket which forced their*

---

[21] Thomas McGuire, *The Surprise of Germantown, October 4, 1777,* (Cliveden of the National Trust for Historic Preservation and Thomas Publications, 1994), 31

[22] Ibid., 31-32

[23] Ibid., 75

Ground, leaving their Baggage.   They retreated a considerable distance....[24]

When General Woodford's brigade finally arrived at Germantown, the sound of combat drew them to the right and away from their column. The 7th Virginia soon found itself at Benjamin's Chew's stone mansion, where an intense struggle for control of the building was underway. Over a hundred British soldiers from the 40th Regiment were barricaded inside the house.[25] The Americans pounded the mansion with cannon fire and stormed it a number of times, but to no avail. The 40th Regiment would not budge, and the ground outside the mansion was littered with American bodies. Although it appears that Woodford's troops did not fire on the house, his four field pieces did.[26] These efforts also failed, however.

Despite this setback, the initial American attack was generally successful. General Sullivan's column swept through the enemy's advance camp with little opposition. Unfortunately, a number of factors soon undermined this success. The morning fog and smoke of battle significantly hampered visibility. As the Americans overran the enemy's lines, they became less orderly. Communication and coordination became very difficult and a tragic case of mistaken identity cost them dearly.

General Anthony Wayne's Pennsylvania brigade had marched several hundred yards past the Chew mansion when they heard the assault on the house. Fearing that the enemy had somehow launched a counter attack in their rear, General Wayne faced about and led his men towards the mansion.

---

[24] "General Washington to John Hancock, 5 October, 1777", *The Papers of George Washington, Vol. 11*, 394

[25] McGuire, 49

[26] Note: Private John Estes of Halifax County noted in his pension application that, "General Woodford's brigade was ordered to retreat before they had fired."
Source: *Virginia Revolutionary Pensions, Vol. 34*, 50

Suddenly, a line of troops emerged through the fog and smoke on their right and fired a volley into their General Wayne's flank. The startled Pennsylvanians responded in kind, unleashing their own volley. Both sides assumed the other was the enemy, but both were mistaken. In the confusion of battle, General Stephen's division, minus Woodford's brigade, fired into Wayne's Pennsylvanians, and Wayne's men fired back. This incident, along with a dwindling supply of ammunition, growing confusion throughout the American line, and a British counter thrust, unraveled Washington's attack and forced the Americans backwards.[27] Washington was shocked by the sudden turn of events. He reported to Congress after the battle that,

> *in the midst of the most promising appearance...when every thing gave the most flattering hopes of victory, the Troops began suddenly to retreat; and entirely left the Field in spite of every effort that could be made to rally them.*[28]

Once again, Washington's army retreated from the field. The attack, which began so promisingly, cost the Americans over 1,000 casualties. The British suffered half that.[29] Yet, despite the loss, the battle of Germantown demonstrated that the American army was still a formidable force. The fall of Philadelphia did not crush America's spirit, as General Howe and the British Ministry had hoped.

---

[27] McGuire, 83

[28] "General Washington to John Hancock, 5 September, 1777", *The Papers of George Washington, Vol. 11*, 394

[29] McGuire, 86-87

Pennsylvania

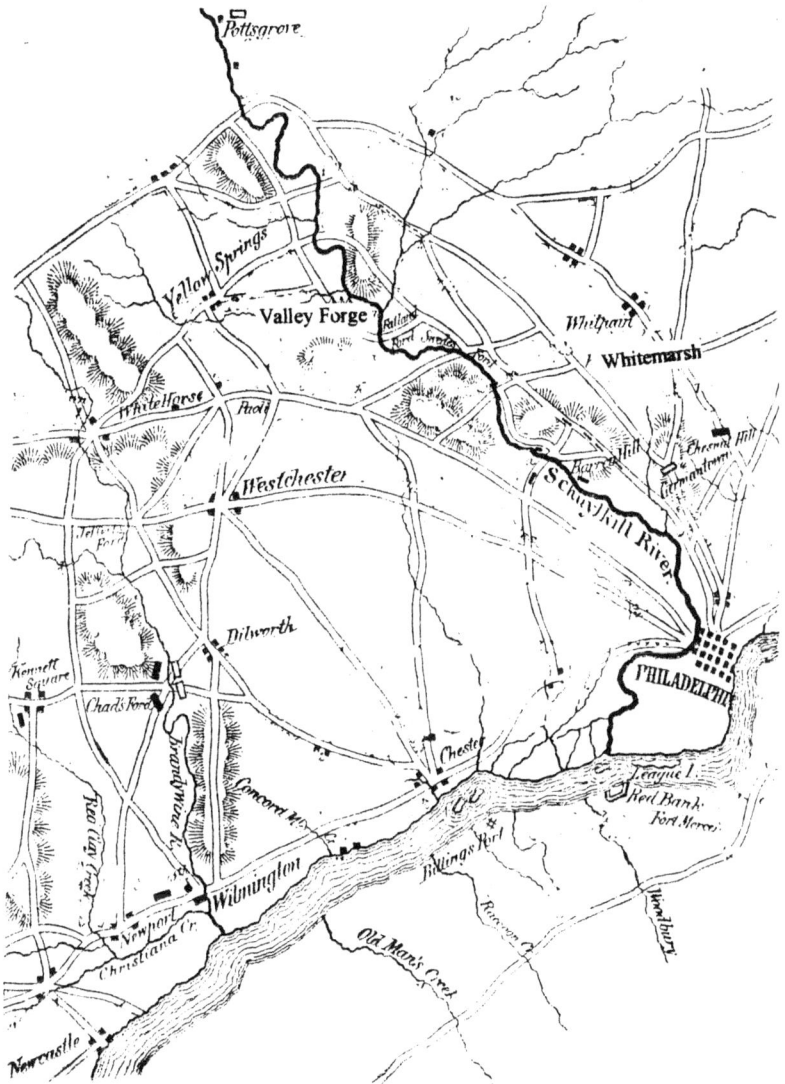

Whitemarsh

General Washington's weary army gradually regrouped outside of Philadelphia. They needed rest and re-enforcements, and General Washington acted to provide both. He informed Congress of his plans on October 7th:

> *My intention is, to encamp the Army at some suitable place to rest and refresh the Men and recover them from the still remaining effects of that disorder naturally attendant on a Retreat. We shall wait here for the Reinforcements coming on, and shall then act accordingly to circumstances.*[30]

While they waited, the Americans addressed some of their deficiencies. A board of officers proposed the following daily rations for the troops:

> *1 ¼ pound of Beef or Salt Fish*
> *or*
> *1 pound Pork*
> *1 ½ pound Flour or Soft Bread*
> *or*
> *1 pound Hard Bread*
> *Half a Gill of Rum or Whiskey per day in lieu of beer*
> *Half a pint of Rice or a pint of Indian Meal per week*
> *3 pounds of Candles to 100 men per week*
> *Soap* [31]

---

[30] "General Washington to John Hancock, 7 October, 1777", *The Papers of George Washington, Vol. 11*, 417

[31] "Board of General Officers, 10 November, 1777", *The Papers of George Washington, Vol. 12*, 188

Officers were reminded that due to a shortage of tents, eight men were assigned to a tent instead of the usual six.[32] General Washington also addressed the shortage of shoes:

> *The commanding officers of corps are immediately to select the most suitable of their men and set them to making Mockasins for their corps....*[33]

Improvements came slowly. Ten days after the order to make moccasins, General Washington lamented to his brother that, *"Our distress on Acct. of Cloathing is great, & in a little time must be very sensibly felt...."* [34]

Such shortages did not prevent Washington from considering another attack. In late October, he solicited the opinion of his officers concerning the feasibility of an attack on Philadelphia. A Council of War rejected this and recommended that the army stay outside the city to harass British foraging parties and patrols. The War Council also stressed the importance of defending the Delaware River forts.[35] These forts blocked British supply ships from sailing to Philadelphia. Fort Mifflin was on an island near the west bank of the river and Fort Mercer was on the east bank in New Jersey.

A considerable amount of General Washington's attention and resources was committed to the forts during October and November. Their defenders waged a heroic fight. On October 22nd, the garrison at Fort Mercer repulsed a strong enemy attack and inflicted heavy losses on the Hessians. At Fort

---

[32] "General Orders, 9 October, 1777", *The Papers of George Washington, Vol. 11*, 452

[33] "General Orders, 8 October, 1777", *The Papers of George Washington, Vol. 11*, 428

[34] "General Washington to Augustine Washington, 18 October, 1777", *The Papers of George Washington, Vol. 11*, 552

[35] "Council of War, 29 October, 1777", *The Papers of George Washington, Vol. 12*, 46-48

Mifflin, the Americans endured a relentless bombardment that literally destroyed the fort.

The 7ᵗʰ Virginia, like most of Washington's army, did not participate in the defense of the river forts. Instead, they camped northwest of Philadelphia and waited for an opportunity to strike. The long period of inactivity affected their conduct and drew critical comments from Washington:

> *Many of the men mount guard daily, who make a very unsoldierlike appearance – The Adjutants & Brigade Majors will be respectfully answerable, that henceforward they bring no man to the parade, whose appearance is not as decent as his circumstances will permit –having his beard shaved – hair combed—face washed – and cloths put on in the best manner in his power.* [36]

Two weeks later, Washington reminded the army that camp fires on sentry duty were not allowed. *"The officers of the day report that Sentries from the picquets keep fires by them – This dangerous practice is absolutely forbidden."* [37]

Below Philadelphia, the British continued their efforts to capture the American river forts. By mid November, the constant enemy bombardment made Fort Mifflin untenable, and the garrison withdrew under cover of darkness. This placed Fort Mercer in an extremely vulnerable position, so it was evacuated two days later. General Howe's supply line to Philadelphia was now open and secure.

While the British worked hard to fortify their position in Philadelphia, the Americans did the same thirteen miles away in the village of Whitemarsh. General Washington hoped for

---

[36] "General Orders, 9 November, 1777", *The Papers of George Washington, Vol. 12*, 177
[37] "General Orders, 21 November, 1777", *The Papers of George Washington, Vol. 12*, 338

another opportunity to attack the enemy and was urged by Congress to do so, but his army simply could not mount a successful attack against Howe's fortified position. Washington settled for small skirmishes with British foraging parties and patrols. Fortunately for the Americans, troops that were ideal for such activity were about to rejoin the army.

Morgan's Corps Returns

Morgan's rifle corps began its long march to Whitemarsh just days after Burgoyne's surrender at Saratoga. General Washington was so eager for its return that he sent his aide, Lieutenant Colonel Alexander Hamilton, to New York to expedite their march. Washington told Hamilton that,

I expect you will meet Colo: Morgan's Corps on their way down, if you do, let them know how essential their services are to us, and desire the Colo...to hasten their March as much as is consistent with the health of the men....[38]

Captain Posey and the rest of Morgan's rifle corps arrived at Whitemarsh in mid November.[39] The unit's numbers were greatly diminished by the hardship of the Saratoga campaign and long march to Pennsylvania. *"There are not more than one hundred and Seventy of Morgan's Corps fit to march, as they in general want Shoes,"* reported General Washington to General Greene.[40]

---

[38] "General Washington to Alexander Hamilton, 30 October, 1777", *The Papers of George Washington, Vol. 12,* 61
[39] "General Washington to General Greene, 22 November, 1777", *The Papers of George Washington, Vol. 12,* 349-350
[40] Ibid.

After a brief rest at Whitemarsh, Morgan's corps joined a large American detachment in New Jersey under General Greene. This detachment was originally intended to assist the garrison at Fort Mercer, but the fort was evacuated prior to their arrival. Despite the loss of Fort Mercer, General Greene remained on the Jersey side of the Delaware River, hoping for an opportunity to strike the enemy. Nothing materialized, so the best Greene could do was send advance parties out to skirmish.

One such party, under the command of the Marquis de La Fayette, engaged the enemy in a sharp skirmish on November 25th. Morgan's riflemen, commanded by Lieutenant Colonel Butler, comprised half of La Fayette's force and greatly impressed him. *"The Marquis is charmed with the spirited behaviour of the Militia & Rifle Corps,"* noted General Greene after the skirmish.[41] La Fayette reported the affair to General Washington and lavished praise on the riflemen:

> *I take the greatest pleasure to let you know that the conduct of our soldiers is above all praises – I never saw men so merry, so spirited, so desirous to go on to the enemy what ever forces they could have as the little party was in this little fight. I found the riflemen above even their reputation...I must tell too the riflemen had been the whole day running before my horse without eating or taking any rest.* [42]

On November 28th, General Greene marched the bulk of his detachment back to Whitemarsh. He left Morgan's corps and Captain Henry Lee's detachment of cavalry in New Jersey

---

[41] "General Greene to General Washington, 26 November, 1777", *The Papers of George Washington, Vol. 12,* 409

[42] "General LaFayette to General Washington, 26 November, 1777", *The Papers of George Washington, Vol. 12,* 418-419

to bolster the militia and harass the enemy.[43] The riflemen spent another week skirmishing with the British. They returned to Whitemarsh in early December, just in time to help fend off General Howe's last major operation of the year.

On the night of December 4th, 10,000 British troops marched towards the American camp at Whitemarsh.[44] The American army, about 12,000 strong, was alerted to the march and manned their fortifications in anticipation of an attack.[45] The British halted at Chestnut Hill, about three miles from Whitemarsh. Washington sent 600 Pennsylvania militia forward to skirmish with Howe's advance parties, but they were easily dispersed.[46] General Howe spent the rest of the day reconnoitering Washington's right wing, looking for a weakness.

By the end of the day, Howe decided that the American defenses on the right were too strong to attack, and he shifted his army three miles east to probe the American left wing.[47] As they approached the American lines, Washington sent Morgan's rifle corps and the Maryland Militia forward to attack their right flank. The engagement was fierce and cost both sides dearly. Captain Johann Ewald, of the German Jagers, recalled that,

The light infantry fell into an ambuscade which the American Colonel Morgan and his corps of riflemen had laid in a marshy wood, through which over fifty men and three officers were killed.[48]

---

[43] "General Greene to General Washington, 28 November, 1777", *The Papers of George Washington, Vol. 12*, 428

[44] David Martin, *The Philadelphia Campaign, June 1777 – July 1778*, (Da Capa Press, 1993), 160

[45] Lesser, "A General Return of the Continental Army...Dec. 3, 1777", 53

[46] Martin, 161

[47] "General Washington to Patrick Henry, 10 December, 1777", *The Papers of George Washington, Vol. 12*, 590

[48] Ewald, 109

Twenty-seven riflemen also fell that day including Major Joseph Morris.[49] This distinguished officer was mortally wounded, and his loss was severely felt by the rifle corps.

General Howe's movements suggested that a major attack was imminent and the Americans braced for combat. The day ended peacefully, however, and the calm continued into the next morning. The British finally moved in the afternoon, but their direction was back towards Philadelphia. General Howe refused to risk his army in an assault on such a strong position; his withdrawal marked an end of the campaign season. The British looked forward to a relatively comfortable winter in Philadelphia. The Americans were not as fortunate.

---

[49] "General Washington to Henry Laurens, 10 December, 1777", *The Papers of George Washington, Vol. 12*, 592

Chapter Five

Valley Forge to Stony Point

On December 19th, General Washington moved his army into winter quarters at Valley Forge. He wanted to keep the army intact and close enough to Philadelphia to challenge enemy incursions into the countryside. Valley Forge was also an excellent site to defend. The Schuylkill River protected the left flank of the Americans and a steep hill, called Mount Joy, covered their rear. Although the front and right flank of the encampment possessed few natural barriers, the open terrain made an attack from those directions very hazardous.

The soldiers constructed log huts as soon as they arrived. They also built two lines of earthworks and redoubts. The outer line extended along a ridge from the Schuylkill River to the foot of Mount Joy. Most of the army was stationed along this line in rows of huts behind the fortifications. An inner defense line was built along Mount Joy. It also ran to the river.

The 7th Virginia and the rest of Woodford's brigade were stationed on the extreme right of the outer line. The earthworks at this location wrapped around a hill, so Woodford's position actually faced west rather than south. The brigade's huts were built at the base of Mount Joy, in a vale that separated them from General Charles Scott's brigade of Virginians.

General Woodford's brigade was a brigade in name only. Its numbers barely reached half the strength of one full regiment, about 350 men, and there were as many men absent due to illness as there were men in camp.[1] Two hundred men

---

[1] Lesser, "A General Return of the Continental Army…December 31, 1777", *The Sinews of Independence*, 54

were unfit for duty because they lacked adequate clothing. The same number, including almost one third of the 7th Virginia (139 men), were granted furloughs as an inducement to re-enlist and were not expected to return until April. When 1779 began, the 7th Virginia had just 30 privates fit for duty. Eighty others were deemed unfit because of inadequate clothing, and 104 were absent due to illness.[2] Even the officer corps was depleted; most of them had returned to Virginia to recruit.

The few 7th Virginians who remained at Valley Forge endured more than a lack of clothing. Provisions were also scarce. On December 22nd, General James Varnum of Rhode Island reported to General Washington that,

> *Three Days successively, we have been destitute of Bread. Two Days we have been intirely without Meat. –It is not to be had from Commissaries. – Whenever we procure Beef, it is of such a vile Quality, as to render it a poor Succedanium for Food. The Men must be supplied, or they cannot be commanded.*[3]

General Washington forwarded the bad news to Congress:

> *I do not know from what cause this alarming deficiency, or rather total failure of Supplies arises: But unless more vigorous exertions and better regulations take place in that line and immediately, This Army must dissolve.*[4]

---

[2] Ibid.

[3] Joseph Lee Boyle, "General Varnum to General Washington, 22 December, 1777," *Writings from the Valley Forge Encampment of the Continental Army, Vol. 1*, (Bowie: Heritage Books Inc., 2000), 2

[4] "General Washington to Henry Laurens, 22 December, 1777", *The Papers of George Washington, Vol. 12*, 667

While the remnants of the 7th Virginia struggled with supply problems at Valley Forge, Captain Posey and the rest of Morgan's riflemen guarded the approaches to camp. They were posted near the village of Radnor, a few miles south of Valley Forge. The riflemen were joined by detachments of cavalry and they skirmished with the enemy all winter.[5]

In January, Colonel Morgan returned to Virginia on furlough. Lieutenant Colonel Butler had already rejoined his regiment. Therefore, command of the rifle corps fell to Captain Posey. Posey recalled in his biography that he,

> *was ordered to take command of the regiment (being the oldest captain) which at this time was very much reduced by the many & repeated actions with the enemy, & hardships & many privations endured. The [rifle] regiment in the course of the insuing spring was engaged in frequent skirmishing on the enemies lines.* [6]

For the 7th Virginians who did not re-enlist and take an early furlough, February was their last month of service. Their departure temporarily eliminated the regiment. Only two privates were present and fit for duty in the 7th Virginia in March, 1778.[7] Over a hundred men were away on furlough. When these men, and the new recruits, arrived in the spring, the regiment's ranks swelled to almost 200 men.[8] They were met by a new commander, Lieutenant Colonel Holt Richeson, one of the regiment's original company captains. He replaced Colonel McClanahan, who resigned in the spring, and

---

[5] Posey Biography
[6] Ibid.
[7] Lesser, "Monthly Return of the Continental Army, March, 1778", 60
[8] Ibid.

Lieutenant Colonel Nelson and Major Cropper who were promoted and transferred to other regiments.[9]

The advent of spring brought improved conditions for the Americans and a change in the routine of camp life, thanks largely to the efforts of a German volunteer named Baron von Steuben. Steuben convinced General Washington to replace the various regional military drills currently practiced in the army, which resulted in confusion on the battlefield, with a uniform system that all the regiments were required to use. The troops spent countless hours learning Steuben's new drill. Gradually, a more professional army developed, one that performed admirably in its first test, the battle of Monmouth.

The Battle of Monmouth

Another European significantly contributed to the American cause in 1778, the King of France. News of America's alliance with France electrified America and altered the strategic situation. Britain had hoped to negotiate a settlement to the conflict that granted America everything it asked, except independence.[10] However, the entry of France into the war ended any hope of a settlement. The Americans were determined to gain complete independence, and with France as an ally, they were confident they could do so.

The war was now a global conflict, which strained Britain's already extended resources to the point that they had to alter their strategy and troop deployments. England's global possessions, especially the valuable Caribbean islands, were vulnerable to French attack. The new British commander in America, General Henry Clinton, was ordered to transfer

---

[9] Sanchez—Saavedra, 51
[10] Martin, 200
    Note: The Conciliatory Acts of March 2, 1778 allowed British
    negotiators to suspend the laws and taxes that Parliament had passed
    to control the colonies.

troops to Florida and the Caribbean, and withdraw from Philadelphia to New York. Preparations for the withdrawal began in May. The tremendous amount of baggage, and large number of loyalist refugees, made it impossible to evacuate everyone by ship. As a result, General Clinton gathered every available wagon, organized an enormous baggage train, and protected it with over 10,000 troops.[11] They left Philadelphia on June 16th and slowly made their way across New Jersey.

General Washington did not interfere with the withdrawal. He was eager for the enemy to leave Philadelphia and did not want to delay their departure, so he only shadowed Clinton's army across New Jersey. Once the British were on the march, Washington looked for an opportunity to strike the British. He ordered Colonel Morgan's rifle corps, augmented to 600 men, to harass the enemy's right flank.[12] Three other large detachments were sent to press Clinton's rear.

On the morning of June 28th, these detachments, under the command of General Charles Lee, engaged the British rear guard near the village of Freehold. The Americans initially did well, but confusing orders issued by General Lee, as well as an aggressive attack by the British, threw the Americans into confusion.

General Washington, who began the day with the main body of the army, was shocked to find his advance troops retreating. After a brief, but heated encounter with General Lee, Washington took command of the troops and rallied a portion of them near a patch of wood. Washington ordered them to delay the enemy's advance as long as possible. General Anthony Wayne recalled that,

[11] Mark M. Boatner III, *Encyclopedia of the American Revolution*, 3rd Ed., (Stanpole Books, 1994), 716
[12] "General Orders, 22 June, 1778", *The Writings of George Washington, Vol. 12*, 106

His Excellency...Ordered me to keep post where he met us...until he had an [opportunity] *of forming the Remainder of the Army and Restoring order – we had just taken post when the Enemy began their attack with Horse, foot, & Artillery, the fire of their whole united force Obliged us after a Severe Conflict to give way....* [13]

Although the Americans at the Point of Wood were quickly overwhelmed, a second American line posted behind a hedge row fence held long enough for Washington to form the main body of the army on a hill in the rear. After the British gained possession of the fence line, a temporary stalemate ensued. Both sides utilized their artillery in an intense duel to drive the other away.

The Americans finally gained an advantage when they placed four cannon on a hill overlooking the left of the British line. The 7th Virginia and the rest of Woodford's brigade played a crucial role in the battle by supporting the four field pieces. The enfilade fire from the battery was so effective that the British were forced to withdraw to a less exposed position. Captain Posey and the rest of Morgan's corps heard the battle, but due to confusing orders, they never joined the fight. They sat three miles away, on the left flank of the British.

The longest battle of the Revolutionary War ended at nightfall. And like the battle of Freeman's Farm, there was no clear victor. Both armies remained on the field, so both claimed victory. When the next day dawned only the American army remained because the British had marched off to Sandy Hook in the middle of the night. General Washington was very pleased with his army and congratulated them in the general orders:

---

[13] "Anthony Wayne to his wife. 1 July, 1778", *The Lee Papers, Vol. 2*, 448-449

The Commander in Chief congratulates the Army on the Victory obtained over the Arms of his Britanick Majesty yesterday and thanks most sincerely the gallant officers and men who distinguished themselves upon the occasion.... [14]

General Washington ordered Morgan's corps to remain near the enemy to prevent them from plundering the countryside while they waited to board ships. [15] The rest of the American army marched to White Plains, New York, about 25 miles north of the city. Washington wanted to maintain a strong presence near the enemy to keep them confined to New York. Both sides settled in for a long standoff.

Prior to their arrival at White Plains, General Woodford's brigade was significantly restructured. This was necessary because all of the regiments in the brigade were seriously undermanned. To remedy this, General Washington ordered Lieutenant Colonel Holt Richeson, the 7th Virginia's commander, to return to Virginia, *"with such Officers of the 3rd, 7th, 11th, and 15th Virginia regiments as can be spared, to superintend the recruiting Service."* [16] The departure of so many officers resulted in the temporary merger of regiments. The 7th regiment was merged with the 3rd which was commanded by Colonel William Heth. The two regiments totaled about 250 rank and file, which was slightly less than the total number of men in the combined 11th and 15th regiments. [17]

---

[14] "General Orders, 29 June, 1778", *The Writings of George Washington, Vol. 12*, 130

[15] "General Washington to Congress, 1 July, 1778", *The Writings of George Washington, Vol. 12*, 146

[16] "General Washington to Lt. Col. Holt Richardson, 1 July, 1778", *The Writings of George Washington, Vol. 12*, 139

[17] Lesser, "A General Return of the Continental Army...August 1, 1778" 78

This arrangement lasted three months, until mid-September, when the entire Virginia Continental Line was re-organized. Under the new arrangement, the original 7th Virginia was renumbered the 5th Virginia, and the original 11th Virginia became the 7th Virginia.[18] The commander of the original 11th Virginia was Colonel Daniel Morgan. He kept that designation throughout his tenure as commander of the rifle corps, so the re-organization of regiments meant that Colonel Morgan was now the commander of the new 7th Virginia regiment.[19]

Morgan's regiment was unique because when it was raised, in early 1777, it had a large number of riflemen in it. Five of the regiment's eight companies were rifle companies (as opposed to the usual three out of ten).[20] The riflemen were raised mainly in Fauqiuer and Frederick County, although one company actually consisted of Pennsylvanians. The three musket companies of the regiment were recruited from Prince William and Loudoun County.[21]

The 11th Virginia was short two companies because four of its original companies never joined the unit. They were captured in 1776 at Fort Washington, New York, months before the 11th Virginia was even formed. To compensate for the missing companies, two new rifle companies were added in the spring of 1777, bringing the total to eight.[22] This was still two companies short of the normal number for Virginia regiments. The quality of the troops and especially the officers made up for the shortage of men. Members of the regiment included: Captains Charles Porterfield and Peter Bruin, who distinguished themselves at Quebec in 1775;

---

[18] Sanchez-Saavedra, 55, 66

[19] Ibid., 53

[20] H.R. McIlwaine, ed. *Journals of the Council of the State of Virginia*, *Vol. 1*, (Richmond: Virginia State Library, 1931), 325

[21] W.T.R. Saffell, *Records of the Revolutionary War*, 3rd Ed. (Baltimore: Charles Saffell, 1894), 260 and Sanchez-Saaedra, 65

[22] Saffell, 256, 260

Captain John Marshall, who was destined to be Chief Justice of the Supreme Court; and of course, Colonel Daniel Morgan.

Posey's Rifle Detachment

Captain Posey was not directly affected by the re-organization of the brigade because he continued to serve with the rifle corps. This unit was considerably reduced in size by battle casualties, fatigue, illness, enlistment expirations, and transfers. By July 1778, the rifle corps had just over a hundred men fit for duty.[23] That was too few for an officer of Colonel Morgan's rank to command, so he took charge of the combined 11th and 15th Virginia regiments. In autumn, Morgan temporarily commanded the entire brigade while General Woodford was home on furlough.

Morgan's departure from the rifle corps did not mean the end of the distinguished unit, however. Command fell to Captain Posey, who was ordered, in mid July, to lead the riflemen to New York and help check the Indians in the state:

The accounts from the Western frontiers of Tyron County are distressing," wrote Washington to Congress on July 22nd, *"The spirit of the Savages seems to be roused, and they appear determined on mischief and havoc, in every Quarter...I have detached the 4th Pennsylvania Regiment and the remains of Morgans corps* [all] *under Lt. Colo. Butler...to co-operate with the Militia and check the Indians if possible.*[24]

---

[23] Richard B. LaCrosse Jr., *Revolutionary Rangers: Daniel Morgan's Riflemen and Their Role on the Northern Frontier,* (Bowie, MD: Heritage Books, 2002), 21
[24] "General Washington to Congress, 22 July, 1778", *The Writings of George Washington, Vol. 12,* 214

While Posey was in New York, he received tragic news from home. His wife, Martha, died as a result of childbirth, and his newborn son soon followed. Posey's two surviving sons, aged five and four, were taken in by Posey's in-laws, and the captain remained with his men.[25]

Captain Posey led numerous expeditions and patrols in New York to suppress the activities of loyalists and their Indian allies. One incursion involved a difficult 300 mile march and resulted in the destruction of a number of Indian settlements.[26] Lieutenant Colonel Butler mistakenly believed that these activities tamed the frontier. He learned otherwise when hundreds of Indians and Tory militia ravaged the Cherry Valley in November.[27]

Butler sent a relief detachment to the area, but it arrived too late to do anything except bury the dead.[28] The approach of cold weather brought an end to combat operations. Winter also marked the end of Posey's service with the rifle corps. On December 20th, General Washington ordered newly promoted Major Thomas Posey to join the 7th Virginia:

> "*Your presence with the Regt. to which you belong is now necessary, you will therefore on the receipt of this repair here.*"[29]

Major Posey found his new regiment comfortably encamped near Middlebrook, New Jersey. The regiment's commander, Colonel Daniel Morgan, commanded General Woodford's brigade during the general's furlough. Lieutenant Colonel John Cropper, the regiment's second in command,

---

[25] Posey Biography

[26] LaCrosse Jr., 33

[27] Ibid.

[28] Ibid., 34

[29] "General Washington to Thomas Posey, 20 December, 1778", *The Writings of George Washington, Vol. 13*, 439

was also away on furlough, so command of the regiment fell to Major Posey.

The approach of winter meant another significant reduction in troops. Colonel Morgan's attempts to stem the loss were largely unsuccessful and he wrote to General Washington with a suggestion:

> *I send you a return of the men enlisted in Gen. Woodford's brigade since the recruiting orders came out...You'll see the number very small; the men are exceedingly backward. For my part, I have used every method in my power, and I thought I had a peculiar turn that way...Numbers would engage if they could get furloughs to go home.*[30]

Like past years, General Washington decided to use furloughs as an incentive for re-enlistments. The policy quickly produced results. When Major Posey rejoined the 7th Virginia in late December, over eighty-five men had been granted furloughs with the promise to return in April.[31] With another twenty-four men absent due to illness, the regiment had less than seventy men fit for duty in camp.[32]

Fortunately for Major Posey and the remaining men in camp, the 1778-79 winter was rather easy and uneventful. Washington's decision to divide the army into several encampments eased the burden of supplying the troops. The smaller encampments did not ravage the local area for provisions like the centralized camp at Valley Forge did. In addition, the weather was mild and General Clinton did very little to threaten or harass Washington's army.

---

[30] Graham, "Col. Morgan to General Washington, 24 November, 1778", 221

[31] Lesser, "Monthly Return of the Continental Army...Dec. 1778", 96

[32] Ibid.

General Woodford returned to his brigade in April, 1779, and watched its ranks slowly grow with new recruits and men returning from furlough. The 7th Virginia nearly tripled its fighting effectiveness by May, 1779, and the army as a whole followed suit.[33] It was once again time for General Washington to prepare for action.

The Light Infantry

With the approach of the 1779 campaign season, General Washington ordered the formation of another corps of Light Infantry. Similar units, such as Morgan's Rifle Corps, and Maxwell's Light Corps, were raised in 1777. General Charles Scott also commanded a separate light corps in 1778.

The Light Infantry Corps of 1779 was different from these. Modeled on the ideas of General Steuben, this unit comprised the best soldiers in the army and served as Washington's shock troops. General Washington ordered the Light Corps' formation on June 12, 1779:

> *The Companies of Light Infantry are to be immediately drawn out...The officers commanding regiments will be particularly careful in the choice of the men, which is a duty, the good of the Service and the credit of their respective regiments equally demand; When it is considered that in every army the honor of a regiment and that of its Light Company are intimately connected, the officers commanding it cannot but be solicitous to furnish men that will support the reputation of the regiment.*[34]

---

[33] Lesser, "Monthly Return of the Continental Army...May 1779", 116

[34] "General Orders, 12 June, 1779", *The Writings of General Washington, Vol. 15*, 265-266

In the same order, General Washington once again re-organized the Virginia line and specified the number of light troops each unit had to contribute. The 2nd, 5th, and 11th Virginia regiments were merged and ordered to contribute a company and a half of light troops (62 men). The 7th Virginia was merged with the 8th Virginia and ordered to send one company of light troops (41 men). All of the chosen men were inspected by the Adjutant General, who was ordered to,

> *pass the men, their clothes, arms, and accoutrements under a critical inspection and return all who on any account shall appear unfit for this kind of service to their regiments to be replaced by others whom he shall approve.*[35]

Three days later, the light infantry troops from Virginia, Pennsylvania, and Maryland were organized into four battalions. Major Posey was placed in command of one of these battalions, which comprised four companies of Virginians. Lieutenant Colonel Fleury, of France, commanded another battalion. Both units were placed under the command of Colonel Christian Febiger. Additional troops from New England and North Carolina were added to the light corps, bringing its number to approximately 1,150.[36]

Command of the light infantry corps was coveted by many officers, including Colonel Daniel Morgan. It went, however, to General Anthony Wayne of Pennsylvania. Morgan took the news hard and resigned his commission. Congress refused to accept his resignation and granted him an indefinite furlough, instead. He returned to Virginia and spent the next fifteen months as a civilian. In the summer of 1780, Congress called Morgan back to service and in January 1781, he added more

---

[35] Ibid.

[36] Don Loprieno, *The Enterprise in Contemplation: The Midnight Assault of Stony Point*, (Westminster MD: Heritage Books, 2004), 21

luster to his distinguished reputation with a smashing victory over Banastre Tarleton at Cowpens.

Stony Point

Both armies limited their activities in the months following the battle of Monmouth. The British, secure behind their fortified lines in New York, conducted occasional foraging details and patrols. After an unsuccessful expedition in Rhode Island, General Washington concentrated the American army near West Point and the New York Highlands. The Americans were too weak to attack New York, but were determined to punish the British whenever they ventured too far into the countryside. To do this, and protect an important Hudson River crossing called King's Ferry, General Washington established fortified posts twelve miles below West Point, at Stony Point and Verplanks.

These posts were seized by the British in early June and significantly strengthened. The garrison at Stony Point numbered over 600 men and was built on a rocky promontory rising 150 feet above the river.[37] It was surrounded by water on three sides and connected to land by a swampy morass that was often submerged at high tide. Two lines of earthworks with abbatis, which were sharp sticks and logs that protruded toward the enemy and acted as barbed wire, were constructed by the British. Several redoubts with cannon were also erected and the post was protected by British ships in the Hudson.

At first glance, Stony Point looked impregnable, but General Washington was determined to re-take it. On July 1st, he ordered General Wayne to conduct a detailed reconnaissance of the fort to determine the feasibility of an attack. Wayne reported his findings to Washington on July 3rd:

---

[37] Ibid., 6-7

I have Reconnoitred the Situation of the Enemy at Stony point & the approaches to them...The sketch herewith transmitted...will give you a General Idea of the Strength of their Works on the West Side which in my Opinion are formidable – (I think too much so for a Storm) [frontal assault] *& to attempt to Reduce it by Regular Approaches* [siege] *will require time as there is no ground within less distance than half a mile but what it commands...Upon the whole I do not think a storm practicable – but perhaps a Surprise may be Effected – could we fall on some stratagem to draw them out.* [38]

Washington embraced General Wayne's idea of a surprise attack, and after gathering more intelligence on the site, recommended the following plan to General Wayne:

My ideas of the enterprize in contemplation are these. That it should be attempted by the light Infantry only, which should march under cover of Night and with the utmost secrecy to the enemys lines, securing every person they find to prevent discovery...the approach should be along the Water on the South side crossing the Beach and entering at the abbatis. This party is to be preceded by a van-guard of prudent and determined men, well commanded who are to remove obstructions, secure the Sentries, and drive in the Guards. They are to advance (the whole of them) with fixed Bayonets and Muskets unloaded...These parties should be followed by the main body at a

---

[38] Charles Stille, "General Wayne to General Washington, 3 July, 1778", *Major-General Anthony Wayne and the Pennsylvania Line in the Continental Army*, (Port Washington, NY: Kenniket Press, Inc., 1968), 186-187 (First published in 1893)

small distance for the purpose of support and making good the advantages which may be gained, or to bring them off in case of repulse and disappointment; other parties may advance to the Works...by the way of the causeway and River on the North...for the purpose of distracting the enemy in their defence as to cut off their retreat. These Parties may be small unless the access and approaches should be very easy and safe. A white feather or Cockade, or some other visible badge of distinction for the night should be worn by our Troops and a watch word agreed on to distinguish friends from foes. [39]

Washington added that General Wayne was free to alter the plan as he saw fit.

On July 15th, the Light Infantry Corps, composed of four regiments totaling about 1200 men, assembled for inspection at Fort Montgomery, eleven miles north of Stony Point. They stood at attention, fully equipped and provisioned, while General Washington reviewed them. They were the cream of the American army, chosen men all, and unaware that they were about to be severely tested.

Instead of returning to camp, like they usually did after such inspections, the light corps marched west and then south, along a heavily wooded and mountainous path. Great lengths were taken to preserve the secrecy of the march. Parties of dragoons patrolled the march route and detained everyone they found for fear that word would reach the enemy of the American advance. This same fear caused General Wayne to keep the destination of the march from his officers.

---

[39] "General Washington to General Wayne, 10 July, 1779", *The Writings of George Washington, Vol. 15,* 396-397

Stony Point

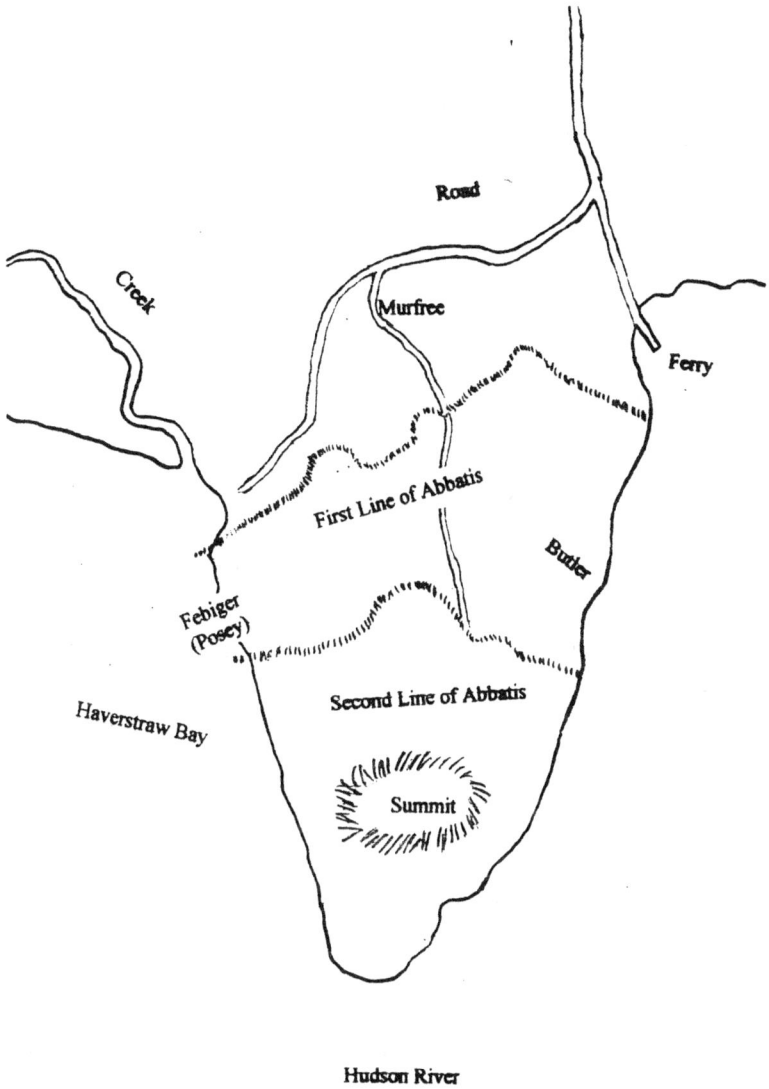

Road

Creek

Murfree

Ferry

First Line of Abbatis

Butler

Febiger
(Posey)

Second Line of Abbatis

Haverstraw Bay

Summit

Hudson River

The Americans finally halted around sunset at Springsteel's Farm, about a mile and a half west of Stony Point. The men rested and refreshed themselves and waited for further orders. Major Posey, who spent the day reconnoitering Stony Point with Major Henry Lee and Captain Allen McLane, reported to General Wayne that nothing was out of the ordinary in the enemy camp.[40]   They appeared to be unaware of the impending attack.

Posey rejoined his battalion and prepared for battle. General Wayne decided to attack at midnight and ordered,

> *Every Officer and Soldier...to fix a Piece of White paper in the most Conspicuous part of his Hat or Cap as an Insignia to be distinguished from the Enemy.*[41]

Wayne's plan called for three detachments to simultaneously attack the fort from three directions. The smallest detachment consisted of two companies of North Carolina troops under Major Hardy Murfree. They were the only troops allowed to load their muskets and were ordered to, *"keep up a perpetual and Galling fire,"* on the center of the enemy's line only after the British pickets became alarmed by the other detachments.[42]   General Wayne hoped that Major Murfree's fire would draw the enemy's attention to the center of their line and away from their flanks.

Lieutenant Colonel Richard Butler, with 300 Maryland and Pennsylvania troops, would assault the northern side of the fort. A twenty man advance party, called a forlorn hope, led the column. Its task was to remove the abbatis and other obstructions for the troops behind them. At the same time,

---

[40] Henry Commager and Richard Morris, ed., "Journal of Captain Allen McLane, 15 July, 1779", *The Spirit of 'Seventy-Six: The Story of the American Revolution as Told by Participants*, (NY: Castle Books, 1967), 732

[41] Stille, "General Wayne's Order of Battle, 15 July, 1779", 402

[42] Ibid., 402

Colonel Christian Febiger and General Wayne led the main American force of 700 men against the southern side of the fort. They planned to wade into Haverstraw Bay to avoid the outer line of abbatis and then charge up the hill to attack the inner works. This force also included a twenty man forlorn hope, commanded by Lieutenant George Knox, as well as a 150 man advance guard led by Lieutenant Colonel Fleury. Major Posey followed behind the advance guard with his battalion. If all went as planned, the light corps would overwhelm the enemy from two directions. The watchword for victory was, *"The fort is ours!"*[43]

The attack began at 12:20 a.m., twenty minutes behind schedule due to high water in the bay.[44] As the Americans approached the fort, British sentries grew alarmed. Although they could not see the Americans, they heard them and fired in their direction. Lieutenant John Ross, the commander of the British picket guard, initially believed that his men were trigger happy and had fired at the wind. A visiting officer asked him what all the commotion was about. Lieutenant Ross recalled,

> *I told* [the officer] *that I saw No Enemy the Night being extremely dark and very Windy, made me suppose that what the Men reported to me to have heard, was occasioned by the Wind rustling amongst the Bushes....* [45]

British sentries on the left side of the line, however, alarmed by the firing of their comrades, soon noticed movement in Haverstraw Bay. It was the main American column,

---

[43] Ibid., and Loprieno, 22
[44] Henry Johnson, "General Wayne to General Washington, 17 July, 1779", *The Storming of Stony Point on the Hudson, Midnight, July 15, 1779: Its Importance in the Light of Unpublished Documents,* (New York: James T. White, 1900), 209
[45] Laprieno, 25

approaching from the south. Simon Davis of the British 17th Regiment noted that he heard,

> *a Noise in the Water on my left which appeared...to have been Occasioned by a large body of Men wading through it....*[46]

The British pickets fired and withdrew to the outer earthworks and braced for an attack. On the left of their line, a twelve pound cannon illuminated the night. Lieutenant William Horndon of the Royal Artillery recalled that,

> *by the light occasioned by the flash of the Gun I could perceive a Body of them* [the Americans] *coming thro' the Water; upon the left... I attempted to bring the Gun to bear upon them, but could not effect it, the Embrazure being too confined.*[47]

Major Posey and the rest of the main American column ignored the activity above them and waded through waist deep water to pass around the enemy's outer abbatis. Lieutenant Colonel William Hull described the advance:

> *The beach was more than two feet deep with water, and before the right column reached it we were fired upon by the out-guards which gave the alarm to the garrison. We were now directly under the fort, and closing in a solid column ascended the hill, which was almost perpendicular. When about half way up our course was impeded by two strong rows of abatis, which the fornlorn hope had not been able entirely to remove. The column proceeded silently on, clearing away the abatis, passed to the*

---

[46] Ibid., 26
[47] Ibid., 176

breastwork, cut and tore away the pickets, cleared the cheveaux de frise at the sally port, mounted the parapet and entered the fort at the point of the bayonet. All this was done under a heavy fire of artillery and musketry, and as strong a resistance as could be made by the British bayonet. [48]

While the main American column scaled the hill and approached the inner works, Major Murfree's small, diversionary, center column engaged the center of the enemy. Murfree successfully occupied a large portion of Colonel Henry Johnson's troops. They were unaware of the American flank attacks and believed that the main attack was directed at the center of the line.

On the American left, Lieutenant Colonel Richard Butler's column successfully swept around the outer abbatis, but it encountered stiff resistance near the inner works. The twenty man forlorn hope party suffered seventeen casualties and the whole column was temporarily pinned down. [49]

On the right, the main American column overcame a brief delay of its own and stormed into the inner works. Colonel Febiger recounted the assault:

Half after eleven o' clock the whole moved forward; the van of the right consisted of 150 volunteers commanded by Lt. Col. Fleury. These were preceded by 20 picked men under the command of Lieut. Knox,...to cover Capt. Shelton, who commanded the front of the remaining 130 men of whom --- men had their muskets slung and carried axes for that purpose; but when Lt. Col. Fleury had taken post with Lieut. Knox in front of the 20 men, and Capt. Skelton finding it impossible to remove the abatis,

---

[48] Johnson, 191
[49] Johnson, "General Wayne to General Washington, 17 July, 1779", 210

and the gallant Major Posey...at the head of Febiger's Regiment pressing close upon him, threw away his axes and took to the Bayonet and followed Fleury and Knox into the works at not more than --- yards distance. [50]

British Lieutenant John Roberts, of the Royal Artillery, described the assault on the fort's inner works from the British perspective:

I heard a Body of them [the Americans] Approaching, and I then concluded that the Enemy were in Possession of the Howitzer Battery, [in front of the inner line] and were pushing for the Upper Work, upon which I also bent my steps that way, but fell over a Log of Wood, and several People fell over me before I recovered myself, and I have great reason to believe that the Enemy entered the upper Work at the Barrier. [51]

Lieutenant Roberts heard cries of *"throw down your arms!"* and discovered that the Americans had also got into the rear of the fort. Convinced that the garrison was lost, he scampered down the hill to Haverstraw Bay and swam to a British ship. Roberts was one of only two British officers to escape.[52]

The battle was not quite over though; Colonel Butler's column was still stalled by enemy resistance, most notably an artillery battery. Major Posey led a party of Americans to silence the battery. He recalled his role in the attack years later:

---

[50] Johnson, 183
[51] Loprieno, 207
[52] Ibid., 208-209

Majr. Posey distinguished himself, being one of the first to enter the main work of the enemy making a charge upon a battery of two 24 [pounders] that was playing upon the left column, [Butler's] that had not reached the fort, in the charge the enemy threw down their arms & cried for mercy, saying spare us brave Americans, spare us spare us, after which there was not a man put to death. [53]

Colonel Febiger's account of the attack supports Posey's recollection. Febiger claimed that just as he captured the British commander Major Posey,

marched across the works and formed where, on the Battery facing north, [Major] Stewart afterwards entered...Colo. Febiger went over to Posey and there saw Capt. Jordon, of Stewart's battalion, just entering the works, which was at least 8 or 10 minutes after Colo. Johnson had surrendered to him, and of course the right column led by Posey had full possession of the Fort previous to even a single man of the left being in. [54]

Colonel Febiger emphasized Posey's role in the attack because he felt that General Wayne slighted Posey and some of the other officers in his after action report to General Washington. Wayne's report, written soon after the battle by the tired and slightly shaken commander suffering from a grazing head wound, omitted Posey's name and described the affair in general terms:

---

[53] Posey Biography
[54] Johnson, 184

it was about twenty minutes after twelve before the assault began -- previous to which I placed myself at the Head of Febiger's Regiment or Right Column & gave the troops the most pointed Orders not to attempt to fire, but put their whole dependence on the Bayonet -- which was faithfully & Literally Observed,-- neither the deep Morass, the formidable & double rows of abbatis or the high & strong works in front & flank could damp the ardor of the troops -- who in the face of a most tremendous and Incessant fire of Musketry & from Artillery loaded with shells & Grape-shot forced their way at the point of the Bayonet thro' every Obstacle, -- both Columns meeting in the Center of the Enemy's works nearly at the same Instant." Too much praise cannot be given to Lieut. Colonel Fleury (who struck the enemy's standard with his own hand) & to Major Steward who Commanded the Advance parties, for their brave & prudent Conduct; Colonels Butler, Meigs & Febiger conducted themselves with that coolness, bravery & perseverance that ever will ensure success. [55]

A few weeks later, responding to complaints from some of the light infantry officers, including Major Posey, that they did not receive the recognition they deserved, General Wayne sent a second report to Congress:

I feel very hurt that I did not in my letter to him [General Washington] of the 17th July, mention (among other brave and worthy officers), the names of Lieut. Col. SHERMAN, Majors HULL, MURPHY and POSEY, whose good conduct and intrepidity justly entitled them to that attention...Permit me,

---

[55] Johnson, 209

therefore, thro your Excellency, to do them that justice now which the state of my wound diverted me from in the first instance.... [56]

Regardless of who deserved the credit, the American attack on Stony Point was a stunning success. The light infantry corps defeated a heavily fortified garrison of nearly 600 men, at the cost of 15 killed and 83 wounded.[57] The British reported approximately 100 men killed or wounded and over 450 captured.[58] This decisive and timely American victory boosted morale throughout the army and reminded the British that the Americans were still a dangerous adversary.

---

[56] Stille, "Wayne's Supplementary Report to the President of Congress, 26 August, 1779", 403-404
[57] Boatner, 1066
[58] Ibid.

Chapter Six

The Southern Campaign

The assault on Stony Point was the light infantry's biggest operation of the year. Although additional fighting occurred in the Wyoming Valley, PA & NY; Vincennes, IN; Paulus Hook, NJ; and Savannah, GA; none of these engagements involved the light infantry corps. Major Posey and the light troops spent the remainder of 1779 encamped on the perimeter of the American army near West Point.[1] Their primary mission was to keep watch for the enemy. This proved to be largely unnecessary as Britain's attention and efforts turned southward. Nevertheless, the light corps conducted frequent patrols and manned the picquet line.

When they were not engaged in such activities, General Wayne had them drilling on the parade ground. Wayne emphasized his high expectations of the light corps in mid-September:

> *The Genl. calls on the officers of this Corps to Pay the strictices & Immediate attention of the menuvering of the troops agreeable to the mode & Rules Laid Down by the Barren Stewben. The officers will Carefully Exammen the State and Condision of the Arms, accutrements, ammunision and Clothing of their respective Comp's and see that Every thing be in Readiness to move at a moment's*

---

[1] *The Orderly Book of Captain Robert Gamble of the Second Virginia Regiment, Commanded by Colonel Christian Febiger, August 21 – November 16, 1779* (Accessed via www.ls.net/~newriver/va/gamble1.html

notis as ...the Eyes of Every Individual will be on the Light Infantry & those Officers & Battalions most esteemed who make the Best appearance on the Parade.[2]

One aspect of the light corps that troubled General Wayne was the lack of uniformity of dress among the men. The light troops were drafted from the various continental regiments and thus, wore a variety of colors and styles. General Wayne wrote to General Washington in mid-September and appealed for more uniformity in the light corps. Washington responded on September 14th :

The Light Infantry being only considered as detachments from the line ought to bear the uniform of the Regiments from which they are taken. Though this from the diversity of our uniforms will not be so favourable to their appearance as might be wished, the contrary would be a deviation from common practice and would not fail to create uneasiness. Besides whenever it should be found expedient to return them to their Regiments it would then produce a more disagreeable diversity in the Regiments to which they belong. [3]

---

[2] "L.I.O (Light Infantry Order) Sept. 18, 1779", in *The Orderly Book of Captain Robert Gamble of the Second Virginia Regiment.*

[3] "General Washington to General Wayne, 14 September, 1779", in *The Writings of George Washington, Vol. 16*, ed. Fitzpatrick (accessed via the Lib. or Congress)

Although he failed to achieve a better look for his light corps, General Wayne continued to emphasize proper conduct and strict discipline among the troops. In mid October, he threatened to assign extra duty to any soldier who was not properly attired and equipped for guard duty:

The Gen'l observes many of the Soldiers who mount Guard Coming on the guard with long Beards & unpowdered & others the powder slovenly put on so therefore Desires the Brigade Maj'r not in futer to [accept] of any Such for Guard or any march without a bayonet but Immediately put them in & on fatigue or Camp Duty in Order to prevent the Loss of Bayonets or other material.[4]

Two days later, General Wayne publicly criticized the Virginia troops about their appearance:

Gen'l Wayne has observed with Great Concern That the Virginians are the only troops in the Light Infantry that has not procurred Hair for their Caps...And Directs the Officers to take the most speedy and Effectual means to procure that Article, no officers to Mount Gard or go on the grand parade Without a Cap, if he had not one of his own, he will [be] kind a nuff to borrow.[5]

And so it went for Major Posey and the light troops for the rest of 1779.

---

[4] "L.I.O. (Light Infantry Order) October 15th, 1779", *The Orderly Book of Captain Robert Gamble of the Second Virginia Regiment.*
[5] Ibid., (October 17th, 1779)

The 7th Virginia in 1779

Posey's regiment, the 7th Virginia, had a relatively uneventful campaign season in 1779. Much of their time was spent in camp (between Middlebrook, New Jersey and West Point, New York). The monotonous camp routine of fatigue duty and drill was occasionally broken by social engagements. Captain John Marshall described one such affair to Major Posey:

Never was I a witness to such a scene of lewdness as about Ramapough particularly at the very venerable Mrs. Sydmon's. I should certainly have thought had I staid there much longer that all the virtue of the fair sex was centered in our Camp Ladies & should very possibly have begun to think of choosing one of them for a Partner for life.[6]

Due to Major Posey's absence, and the resignations of Colonel Morgan and Lieutenant Colonel Cropper, (who had re-joined the "new" 7th Virginia under the White Plains Arrangement), the 150 men of the 7th Virginia were temporarily commanded by Major William Croghan of the 8th Virginia.[7]

In late October, reports of enemy movements triggered a flurry of activity. Woodford's brigade was ordered to march from Kakeate, New York, to Springfield, New Jersey.[8] Woodford reported on his progress to General Stirling.

---

[6] Charles Cullen and Herbert A. Johnson, ed., "John Marshall to Thomas Posey, 1 September, 1779", *The Papers of John Marshall, Vol. 1*, (Chapel Hill : Univ. of NC Press, 1974), 34

[7] Ibid., 37; and Lesser, "Monthly Return of the Continental Army for Sept., Oct., & Nov., 1779", 132, 136, 140

[8] Catesby Willis Stewart , "General Woodford to General Stirling, 26 October, 1779", *The Life of Brigadier General William Woodford of The American Revolution, Vol. 2*, (Richmond, VA: Whittet & Shepperson, 1973), 1100.

> *Upon the alarm of the Enemies coming into this state,*
> *I marched the Division to Sufferans where I left all*
> *our Tents and Baggage, with a guard of lame and*
> *bare footed men under command of Maj. Clarke....*[9]

Nothing came of the alarm, so Woodford's brigade returned to Kakeate. They remained there for about a week and then marched to Haverstraw, New York, just below Stony Point.[10]

After things settled down, Colonel John Neville of the 4th Virginia regiment wrote to Colonel Morgan with news of Woodford's brigade. The letter highlighted the esteem in which Morgan was still held by his peers and his men:

> *We have been imployed [some] Time in Making*
> *Fashions [facines] and Gabions upon which the*
> *Enemy left Stony and Planks Point, we are*
> *Rebuilding a small Part of it which must be a Post for*
> *some Poor field officer this winter...Genl. Woodford*
> *has had the Command of this Division for some time*
> *Past and am Sorry to inform you he is very Much*
> *Disliked in Perticular By his Old Brigade Much more*
> *than By those that joined him this Campaign for my*
> *Part I would wish never to Part with him & the Old*
> *Lord [Stirling]. However officers are willing to a*
> *man and wish to hear of his Promotion to a Majr.*
> *Genl. Then says they for old Morgan a Brig. And we*
> *will kick the world before us. I am not fond of*
> *Flattery but I assure you on my word No Man Ever*
> *Leaving the army was more Regretted than yours nor*
> *no man Ever wished for More to Return.*[11]

---

[9] Ibid., "General Woodford to General Stirling, 28 Oct. 1779", 1103

[10] Ibid., "General Woodford to General Washington, 9 Nov. 1779", 1108

[11] Ibid., "Col. John Neville to Col. Daniel Morgan, 9 Nov. 1779", 1114

The 7th Virginia and the rest of the brigade stayed in Haverstraw for two weeks. On November 21st, General Washington ordered the Virginians to march to Morristown to prepare winter quarters.[12] Two weeks later, with reports of a planned enemy expedition in the south, Washington ordered the entire Virginia line to march to South Carolina to assist the American forces there. On December 8th he informed General Woodford that,

> *I have this minute been honoured with a Letter from Congress directing the Troops of the Virginia line to be put in motion immediately. You will put every thing in train and march the whole, with their Tents and baggage as soon as possible to Philadelphia, where you will receive further Orders from Congress...The Officers and Men of the line with the light Infantry, I shall order to proceed to Philadelphia and join their respective Regiments.*[13]

As directed in this order, Major Posey and the rest of the Virginia light troops rejoined their original units near Philadelphia and prepared to march south.

---

[12] "Gen. George Washington to Gen. William Woodford, 21 Nov. 1779", *The Writings of George Washington*, edited by John C. Fitzpatrick, (accessed via the Library of Congress website)
[13] Ibid., "Gen. Washington to Gen. Woodford, 8 Dec. 1779"

The March South

Preparations for the long march proved more difficult than anticipated. Since it made little sense to march soldiers to South Carolina whose enlistments were about to expire, efforts to re-enlist the men were renewed. On December 15th, Congress decreed that,

> *such of the Virginia troops whose times of service will expire by the last day of March next, and who incline to inlist for the usual bounties, to serve during the war, be permitted to go home on furlough till the first day of April next....*[14]

Only a handful of troops re-enlisted and received furloughs, however.[15] Those Virginians whose service expired in the spring remained with the main army until their discharge date. An exception was made for 213 men whose service ended on December 31st. These men escorted enemy prisoners to Fort Frederick, Maryland, and then marched home.[16]

Originally, General Woodford hoped to spare his men from part of the march by sailing from Head of Elk, Maryland to Williamsburg, Virginia. Unfortunately, this could not be arranged so the Virginians prepared to march the entire way. General Woodford was troubled by the change and expressed his concern to General Washington:

> *I expect the whole will get from Philadelphia early in the next week. We are ordered the rout of Lancaster, York, Frederick Town, etc. Orders have been sent to*

---

[14] Journal of Congress, 15 December, 1779
(Access via the Lib. of Congress website at www.loc.gov)
[15] Lesser, "Monthly Return of the Continental Army...for January, 1780" 148
[16] Journal of Congress, 15 December, 1779

the different Posts, to make the necessary provisions for us, but if I am to judge from the present state of the several departments at Phila. I fear there will be no certainty of being supplied. I see many difficulties in the long march of land at this season.... [17]

General Woodford proposed to Washington that the Virginia continental troops, numbering roughly 1,500 men, be organized into three battalions. General Washington gave his approval on December 24th :

I think the forming the Men that are to go with you into three Battalions, as you propose, an eligible plan, and I doubt not but you will do it in such a way with respect to the Officers, as will be most agreeable. [18]

Although it is difficult to determine the total number of 7th Virginians who marched to Charleston, at least one company from the regiment, under Captain James Wright, was attached to Colonel William Russell's battalion. [19]

In mid-January, more than a month after they were ordered to march south, General Woodford and his men were still in Pennsylvania. He explained the cause of the delay to General Washington:

---

[17] Stewart, "Gen. Woodford to Gen. Washington, 28 Dec. 1779", 1136-37
[18] "Gen. Washington to Gen. Woodford, 20 Dec. 1779", *The Writings of George Washington, Vol. ,* and A Return of the Continental Army…for January, 1780, in Lesser, 148
[19] Sanchez-Saavedra, 179
See also: Pension applications for James Brown and William Berkley in, Dorman, *Virginia Revolutionary Pension Applications, Vol. 11,* 41 and *Vol. 6,* 60 respectively

The extreme badness of the weather had detained the troops much longer here than I could have expected. Together with the difficulty of getting them supplied with necessaries for so long a march by land, they are still deficient in blankets, breeches, and shirts for other things are tolerably well off. The two divisions under Colo. Russell and Neville with the artillery are by this time at or near Lancaster; the third and last division marched this day and tomorrow I shall leave town to get with the front and after giving the necessary orders shall proceed to Fredericksburg to make provision for their reception. It was thought best by the Board of War to march them separately this severe weather for the convenience of accommodating them with quarters but by the time they reach Fredericksburg should hope it will be more moderate that the tents may be pitched and the troops move in a body, which will contribute much to good order and discipline.[20]

On February 8th, General Woodford reported his progress to Washington:

The first and second division of the troops arrived at this place; [Fredericksburg] the third under the command of Colo. Gist will not be here in less than five or six days, the fatiguing march the troops have had this extreme bad weather, the reduced situation of the wagons and artillery, Horses, together with sundry repairs wanting to the wagons, had induced me to halt them here till the rear gets up—when I shall put them in motion for Petersburg. The continuance of the frost will oblige me to march still by divisions, this is much against my inclination if it

---

[20] Stewart, "Gen. Woodford to Gen. Washington, 13 Jan. 1779", 1144

121

could be avoided, but without this method it would be impossible to provide quarters for the officers and men in this country. There has been some desertions, but not so considerable as I feared. We have picked up some recruits and shall continue to do all we can in that way...The troops have been healthy till lately. Several have been taken ill and I fear the number of our sick will increase.[21]

The march slowed considerably between Fredericksburg and Petersburg as wet weather made the roads nearly impassable. On March 8th, General Woodford sheepishly updated General Washington:

My last to your Excellency was from Fredericksburg the 8th of February. You will no doubt be surprised that we should be near a month in getting so short a distance—but you may be assured it was not possible to get the artillery and baggage on one day sooner and if it had not been for the assistance we received from the Gentlemen upon the road, they would not have reached this till the Earth was settled. The day I arrived here [Petersburg] I received a letter from Gen'l Lincoln...this determined me to leave my artillery stores and baggage to follow on. The troops marched this morning. I took on a few wagons to carry our tents as I could not think it prudent to expose the men upon so long a march. The artillery will leave this in a few days – escorted by 140 men of Colo. Buford's regiment which is all of that corps who can be marched at present, about 300 of them will be left and I see no probability of them being equipt for a march in any short time. General Scott is here at present, but will go on without the men in a

---

[21] Ibid., "Gen. Woodford to Gen. Washington, 8 Feb. 1779", 1148-49

few days...I am sorry to inform your Excellency that our numbers are much reduced by desertion and sickness together with the furloughed men....[22]

The final push to Charleston began soon after this letter. With better weather and roads, Woodford's men marched 500 miles in thirty days and arrived in Charleston on April 7th. General Woodford wrote to General Washington the next day.

After a forced march of five hundred and five miles, which we performed in thirty days, I had the pleasure of throwing my troops into town in good health and spirits, by the only passage now left open. We arrived on the 7th at two o'clock, to the great joy of the garrison.[23]

Siege of Charleston

Charleston, the south's largest town, had long been a target of the British. Attempts to capture it in 1776 and 1779 failed, but General Clinton hoped that one last effort would do the trick. In late December 1779, a floatilla of ships with thousands of British soldiers left New York bound for Charleston. General Clinton and his troops landed on the Carolina coast in early February and gradually advanced toward the town.

At the time of Clinton's arrival Charleston was defended by approximately 3,600 American troops. Less than half of them, (about 1,600) were continental soldiers from South

---

[22] Ibid., "Gen. Woodford to Gen. Washington, 8 March, 1779", 1154-55

[23] Jared Sparks, ed., "Gen. Woodford to Gen. Washington, 8 April, 1779", *The Correspondence of the American Revolution being Letters of Eminent Men to George Washington, Vol. 2* (Boston : Little, Brown & Co., 1853), 430

Charleston

Carolina and Virginia. The rest were militia from North and South Carolina.[24] The garrison was re-enforced in early March by 600 North Carolina continentals.[25] Unfortunately, in mid-March, 700 North Carolina militia departed when their term of service expired.[26]

General Benjamin Lincoln, a veteran of Saratoga, commanded the garrison. The Americans hoped that their extensive array of earthworks, redoubts, and obstacles, which stretched across the Charleston peninsula from the Ashley to the Cooper River, would defeat any land assault on the town. They also believed that the difficult navigation of Charleston harbor, combined with the cannon of Fort Moultrie, which guarded the passage to the harbor, would repulse any attack by sea.

British General Henry Clinton was determined to take Charleston, however, and on March 29th, his army crossed the Ashley river and camped on Charleston Neck, just a few miles above the American lines. On April 1st, three thousand British soldiers, half armed with muskets and half armed with entrenching tools, advanced towards the Americans. They broke ground on their first parallel (siege line) that evening. The line, which eventually extended across the peninsula, was between 800 and 1000 yards away from the American line.[27]

When the Americans discovered the British activity, they rushed more cannon to their lines and commenced a heavy bombardment. Although the cannonade slowed British work parties and harmed a few soldiers, it was mostly ineffective. Since their own artillery batteries were not completed, the British could only respond with cannon fire from across the Ashley River. Nonetheless, these shots, which hit the town instead of the American lines, caused great concern in

---

[24] Boatner, 208
[25] Patrick O'Kelly, *Nothing But Blood and Slaughter: The Revolutionary War in the Carolinas*, (Blue House Tavern Press, 2004), 61
[26] Ibid., 66
[27] Ibid., 121

Charleston. Captain Johann Ewald of the German Jagers described the town's reaction:

> *A terrible clamor arose among the inhabitants of the city, since the firing came entirely unexpectedly...I could often hear the loud wailing of female voices, which took all the pleasure out of my curiosity and moved me to tears.*[28]

Charleston's fear and anxiety significantly decreased on April 7th, when General Woodford's Virginia continentals arrived. Church bells rang, cannon fired a salute, and the townsfolk cheered the Virginians as they marched through the town and went straight to the American lines.[29]

The joy generated by General Woodford's arrival was cut short the next day by bad news from Fort Moultrie. The British navy successfully sailed past the fort with minimal damage. Although Charleston's shore batteries still protected the town from a sea borne assault, the noose nevertheless, tightened around Charleston .

General Clinton believed that the siege had progressed far enough to justify a summons to the Americans for their surrender. The demand was delivered under a flag of truce on April 10th and promptly dismissed. Although General Lincoln flatly rejected General Clinton's summons, the American commander was concerned. Lincoln held a council of war with his officers on April 13th, to discuss the army's situation. Some of the officers proposed that they evacuate Charleston.[30] Discussion was cut short when British cannon suddenly opened fire on the American lines. The officers hastily

---

[28] Ewald, 224-225

[29] Carl P. Borick, *A Gallant Defense: The Siege of Charleston, 1780,* (University of South Carolina Press, 2003), 129-130

[30] Ibid., 139

returned to their posts and endured a twelve hour artillery barrage.

In the evening, the British began to dig a second parallel only 300 yards from the American line.[31] They also sent a force across the Cooper River to threaten Charleston's last communication and supply link to the north. This link was partially defended by a small American force of two hundred men under Colonel Francois Malmedy.[32] They held a fortified position at Lamprier's Point, on the east bank of the Cooper River.

Monck's Corner

Colonel Malmedy's detachment was not the only American force east of the river. General Isaac Huger screened the upper part of the river near Monck's Corner with approximately 400 cavalry and militia.[33] As long as the Americans held Monck's Corner and Lamprier's Point, an avenue of escape remained, and vital supplies and reinforcements could reach Charleston.

On the evening of April 13th, British Lieutenant Colonel Banastre Tarleton advanced toward's Monck's Corner with a detachment of cavalry to sever this link to the north. They arrived before dawn, overwhelmed the lone American patrol posted on the road, and charged into the startled American camp. Colonel Tarleton described the attack:

At three o'clock in the morning the advanced guard of dragoons and mounted infantry, supported by the remainder of the legion and Ferguson's corps,

---

[31] Borick, 161; and Captain Johann Hinrichs, *The Siege of Charleson: Diaries and Letters of Hessian Officers*, trans. & ed. Bernhard A. Uhlendorf, (Ann Arbor: University of Michigan Press, 1938), 249
[32] Borick, 144
[33] Ibid., 148

approached the American post; a watch word was immediately communicated to the officers and soldiers, which was closely followed by an order to charge the enemy's grand guard on the main road...and to pursue them into their camp. The order was executed with the greatest promptitude and success. The Americans were completly surprised... many officers and men, fled on foot to the swamps, close to their encampment, where being concealed by the darkness, they effected their escape; Four hundred horses...fell into the hands of the victors; about one hundred officers, dragoons, and hussars, together with fifty waggons, loaded with arms, clothing, and ammunition, shared the same fate. [34]

In addition to these losses, the Americans suffered fifteen dead and eighteen wounded. Only one of Tarleton's men was killed and two others wounded.[35]   Colonel Tarleton's aggressive tactics had smashed the American cavalry.

The British received more good news on April 18th when 2,500 reinforcements arrived from New York.[36]   Their arrival allowed General Clinton to send more men across the Cooper River to tighten his grip there.   General Cornwallis took charge of 2,300 men and positioned them to oppose an American retreat from Charleston, if one occurred.   He also tried to restrict supplies from reaching the town.   This proved difficult, because the Americans still held Lamprier's Point, and General Cornwallis was unable to block every avenue to the post.[37]

---

[34] Banastre Tarleton, *A History of the Campaigns of 1780-1781 in the Southern Provinces of North America*, (NH: AYER Company, 1999),   16 Originally printed in 1787

[35] Borick,   149 and Tarleton,   17

[36] Borick,   158

[37] Ibid.,   159; 182-184

General Lincoln, aware of the importance of Lamprier's Point, sent Lieutenant Colonel Henry Laurens with 300 men, including the garrison's light infantry troops, to bolster its defense.[38] These reinforcements, in conjunction with the strong earthworks of the post, dissuaded General Cornwallis from launching a direct assault on the position.[39]

In Charleston, the Americans continued to bombard British work parties and inflict casualties, but the enemy steadily crept forward. Captain Ewald described the intensity of the American fire:

The fire of the besieged was extraordinary: they fired scrap iron and broken glass. Although this fire is not very dangerous, and the fragments usually fly up in the air, my men lost their composure and thought of nothing else but to conceal themselves....[40]

The British completed their second parallel in mid-April, despite the hot fire of the Americans, and immediately began work on a third. Captain Ewald noted that,

We have now approached so close that one could easily throw a stone into the advanced ditch on the other side, which is dressed with pointed trees. I occupied the heads today, and was kept warm with stone missiles and scrap iron.[41]

The two armies were within musket range of each other, which made life in the trenches even harder. Grueling work in the heat and mud under frequent bombardment and deplorable conditions was the norm for the men on both sides. With just

---

[38] Ibid., 183
[39] Ibid., 185
[40] Ewald, 231
[41] Ibid., 232

a few hundred yards separating the two sides, the ever-present danger of small arms fire added to the misery of trench warfare. Losses mounted in both armies.

Casualties did not alarm General Lincoln as much as the army's dwindling supplies. On April 20th, Lincoln held another war council to discuss the situation. The garrison's food supply and ordinance was running low, and there was significant doubt whether they could hold the town much longer. Some of the officers again proposed an evacuation of the town. While this was debated, a few of Charleston's civilian leaders arrived and joined the discussion. They strenuously objected to an evacuation and threatened to turn against the American army and assist the enemy if a withdrawal was attempted. These objections ended the discussion, and the council adjourned with nothing resolved.

Four days after the council meeting, General Lincoln surprised the enemy with an early morning bayonet attack by two hundred Virginia and South Carolina continentals.[42] Captain Ewald described the affair:

> *The enemy attack was made with bayonet in hand, without firing a shot. The [British] light infantry abandoned a part of their post and rushed back to the second parallel, whereby the jagers had to pay for the feast. Since it was not yet daylight and they could not shoot, the jagers defended themselves with their hunting swords. Two jagers were bayoneted, four severely wounded, and two, along with eight Englishmen, were captured.[43]*

---

[42] Borick, 177-178
[43] Ewald, 233

The impact of the attack extended into the next evening when American sentries, firing into the dark, alarmed British troops in the third parallel. Afraid that another sortie was underway, the British fled to the rear towards the second parallel. The troops there were just as anxious and fired at their retreating comrades under the mistaken belief that they were Americans. The truth was that no one had left the American lines.[44]

The British were not the only ones embarrassed by false information, however. On April 27th, Colonel Malmedy, at Lamprier's Point, received news that a large enemy force was en route to attack his post. Malmedy believed that his detachment, which was reduced to just 100 continentals and 200 militia, was no match for the British and he hastily withdrew across the river.[45] The last avenue of escape, supply, and communication for the Americans was abandoned to the enemy without a fight.

Three days later the British siege lines reached the first obstacle of the American line, a canal cut across the peninsula.[46] The water was drained and the British continued forward, towards the abbatis and outer wall of the American line. On May 7th more bad news befell the Americans when Fort Moultrie surrendered.[47] Although the fort's military importance had significantly diminished after the British navy slipped past it in April, Fort Moultrie remained a symbol of resistance, and its capture was another blow to the Americans.

General Clinton hoped that these developments had weakened his adversary's resolve and that General Lincoln would re-consider capitulation. On May 8th, he once again summoned the garrison to surrender. A two day cease fire ensued as letters were exchanged about the terms of a

---

[44] Borick, 178-179
[45] Ibid., 187-189
[46] Ewald, 234
[47] Borick, 206

surrender. Disagreement over the status of the militia and civilians of Charleston undermined the negotiations, and a massive discharge of artillery and musket fire from both sides signaled the resumption of hostilities. Captain Johann Hinrichs of the German jagers described the action:

> *At eight o'clock the armistice was over. The enemy rang all the bells in the city and after a threefold Hurray! Opened a cannonade more furious than any before...In the morning our guns and howitzers opened a murderous fire...The cannonade lasted the entire day, and during the night a great number of shells were thrown.* [48]

Despite General Lincoln's determination to hold out for better terms of surrender, the will to resist among his men, (especially the militia), was largely gone. Some of the militia abandoned their post and over 500 petitioned General Lincoln to accept Clinton's terms. Even the civilian leaders of Charleston, who were so adamant about the army fighting to the last, pleaded with General Lincoln to surrender the town.[49] With supplies dwindling, morale plummeting, and hope of relief non-existent General Lincoln decided that further resistance was futile. He informed General Clinton on May 11th that the terms of capitulation were accepted, and the Americans formally surrendered the next day.

Considering the duration of the siege, and the amount of ordinance expended by each side, casualties were surprisingly light. Over 300 British troops were killed or wounded, and approximately 240 Americans were lost.[50] Many more Americans died after the surrender aboard prison barges in

---

[48] Captain Hinrichs, in *The Siege of Charleston*, trans & ed. Bernhard Uhlendorf, 287
[49] Borick, 216-217
[50] Borick, 222

Charleston harbor. Over 5,000 Americans surrendered at Charleston, including the bulk of the Virginia continental line.[51]

Although Charleston marked the last time members of the 7th Virginia fought as 7th Virginians, it did not mark the end of the regiment's contribution to the war effort. Individual members of the 7th, scattered in units from Virginia to South Carolina, continued to fight. The pension applications of numerous 7th Virginians claim participation in the battles of Camden, Cowpens, Guilford Courthouse, Yorktown and others. One of the 7th Virginians who continued to fight was Major Thomas Posey.

---

[51] Ibid., 222-223

Chapter Seven

Posey's Battalion

Major Posey arrived in South Carolina too late to join the besieged garrison in Charleston; the enemy controlled all lines of communication to the town. He watched helplessly as the British pounded the Americans into submission. When the garrison surrendered, Posey offered his services to South Carolina's governor, John Rutledge. The Governor informed Posey that there were no troops to lead, *"the militia could not be collected, the inhabitants* [were] *flying in all directions."*[1]

Major Posey returned to Virginia without a command. He spent the rest of the year recruiting, unsuccessfully, in the Shenandoah Valley.[2] In December 1780, Virginia was greatly alarmed by the arrival of 1,200 British troops under the infamous traitor, Benedict Arnold.[3] The state government pleaded for troops, and in mid-January Major Posey accompanied his late wife's uncle, Colonel Sampson Mathews, and 250 Augusta County militia on a march eastward. They were ordered to Fredericksburg to protect the vital supply depot from a possible raid.[4]

General Arnold did not stray from the James River, however. He was content to wreak havoc within supporting distance of the British navy. In February, Arnold withdrew to Portsmouth and the crisis abated.

---

[1] Posey Biography

[2] John Thornton Posey,

[3] Boatner, 1149

[4] "Sampson Mathews to Thomas Jefferson, 13 January, 1781", *The Papers Thomas Jefferson, Vol. 4*, ed. Julian Boyd (Princeton, NJ: Princeton University Press, 1951), 350

By March, Major Posey was back in the Shenandoah Valley struggling to recruit men. His frustration led him to complain to Colonel William Davies that men who were "*well adapted to military service*" were turned away because they did not meet the minimal height requirement of five feet four inches.[5]

Posey's frustration continued into May, when, despite his best efforts, only 21 men enlisted.[6] A draft was implemented, but resistance to it was very high. Major Posey described some of the resistance to Colonel Davies:

> *The draft for eighteen monthers, has not yet taken place, in any of these back Counties...The people seem much averse to it in Augusta & Rockbridge, but it don't amount to a majority I beleave. However, a considerable number met at the places appointed for laying of the Districts, & in a very bold & daring manner, seased the papers and destroyed them. I don't know where this may stop, if there is not a timeous check, in Hanging a few, for examples to the rest...I have a deserter or two delivered to me every five or six days – I suppose I shall have a compy of them in a short time to send down.[7]*

The reluctance to serve was disturbing, especially given that Virginia was under attack again. Over 7,000 British soldiers, commanded by General Cornwallis, were in the state.[8] General Washington sent Generals Steuben, LaFayette,

---

[5] "Thomas Posey to Col. William Davies, 27 March, 1781", *Calendar of Virginia State Papers, Vol. 1*, ed. William Palmer, (Richmond: R.F. Walker, 1875), 603

[6] Ibid., 602

[7] "Thomas Posey to Col. William Davies, 18 May, 1781", *Calendar of Virginia State Papers, Vol. 2*, 107

[8] Boatner, 1152

and Wayne, with continental reinforcements, to Virginia, but they were unable to check the enemy.

This dramatically changed in late September when a combined American and French army, under General Washington and General Rochambeau, trapped General Cornwallis at Yorktown. Posey, who was promoted to Lieutenant Colonel that summer, did not actively participate in the siege of Yorktown, but he arrived in time to witness the enemy's surrender:

> *in the time of the siege of Little York [I] was there, & had the pleasure of beholding another large British force surrender to the American arms.*[9]

Although he only played a small role at Yorktown, Thomas Posey could proudly boast that he participated in the two biggest British defeats of the war.

While Britain's defeat at Yorktown was a severe blow to the ministry's efforts to retain the colonies, it did not immediately end hostilities. The British still held New York, Charleston, and Savannah, as well as a number of smaller posts. General Washington wanted to keep pressure on the enemy, so he sent reinforcements from Virginia to General Nathaniel Greene in South Carolina. Lieutenant Colonel Posey was selected to lead the detachment but an outbreak of small pox and a serious supply shortage delayed the march for months.

When smallpox was discovered in camp, Colonel Christian Febiger, the overall commander of the Virginia continental forces at Cumberland Old Court House, decided to postpone Posey's departure and inoculate the troops. Significant resistance to the inoculations from local inhabitants, who feared that the disease would spread to them, undermined Febiger's plan. The locals threatened to withhold much

---

[9] Posey Biography

needed provision, if the inoculations occurred. Colonel Febiger also lacked adequate supplies for the inoculations. These obstacles frustrated Febiger to the point that he canceled the inoculations.[10]

Colonel Febiger was soon confronted with another obstacle that delayed the march. In mid-November, Lieutenant Colonel Posey and some of the officers of his detachment reported to Colonel Febiger that they lacked the necessary supplies to conduct the march:

Dear Colonel,

The officers at this Station, understanding a Detachment is shortly to march from here to the Southward, Beg leave...to lay before you their Incapacity for undertaking such an expedition...we are destitute of Cash...We are truly destitute of cloathing...We wish to render our Country every service in our power. We have done it, tho' with the loss of health and fortune, and are still agreed and ready to march...if supply'd in any suitable manner, but we cannot in justice to ourselves, under such circumstances, yield the submission and pursue the same schemes now, when there is not the same necessity as heretofore, but must observe to our Rulers, how ungenerously, nay how inhumanely they have treated us....[11]

Posey and the other officers threatened to resign rather than march south under such difficult conditions.

---

[10] "Col. Christian Febiger to Gov. Nelson, 16 November, 1781", *Calendar of Virginia State Papers, Vol. 2*, 602

[11] "Col. C. Febiger to Col. Davies, 17 November, 1781", *Calendar of Virginia State Papers, Vol. 2*, 609

This bold letter gained mixed results for Colonel Posey and his men. General Washington appealed to Virginia's governor to intervene and send more supplies to the detachment.[12] On the other hand, Washington was very displeased by Posey's action, which he believed undermined discipline in the ranks. He expressed his displeasure to Colonel Febiger:

> *The impropriety of such conduct...is so glaring, that I am in hopes the Gentlemen will upon cool reflection condemn it themselves. What can they expect from their soldiers, when they themselves strike at the Root of Authority and discipline? That they have reason to complain, in common with their Brethren, of the hardships they have indured and the difficulties they labor under for want of their pay, I am ready to allow; but they are mistaken if they thing they are the only sufferers.*[13]

Washington told Colonel Febiger to inform the disgruntled officers that greater efforts to supply them were forthcoming. At the same time he expressed his expectation that the detachment march as soon as possible:

> *I shall be very anxious to hear from you on the subject,"* Washington concluded, *"for you must suppose my feelings are particularly wounded on the occasion. When asked whether any and what reinforcements have marched from Virginia, I shall blush when I say none, and more so when I assign the cause.*[14]

---

[12] "General Washington to Governor Benjamin Harrison, 10 January, 1782", *The Writings of George Washington, Vol. 23*, 436
[13] "General Washington to Colonel Christian Febiger, 12 January, 1782", *The Writings of George Washington, Vol. 23*, 443
[14] Ibid., 444

General Washington's subtle rebuke of Colonel Posey greatly distressed him and prompted him to action.[15] On February 14th, 1782, Posey's 400 man detachment paraded at Cumberland Old Court House. Many of the men still lacked adequate supplies, and there was a lot of grumbling in the line. Colonel Posey described the affair in a letter:

> *On the 14th late in the day, we set out from C.O.C.H.* [Cumberland Old Court House]. *I was under some apprehentions a little before our march, that the men would prove refractory, for which reason the whole of the Officers put themselves in readiness for action; upon which the men seeing a determined and steady carriage among the officers, they declined putting into execution their concerted scheme.*[16]

Colonel Febiger's account of the affair was more detailed:

> *On the 14th inst: I gott rid of the said Detachment, after hanging one and whipping 73 of them, and they are well officer'd & Posey informs me behave well on their march. I dismounted the Officers, which has a good Effect.*[17]

Although the march was plagued by bad weather and roads, a lack of provisions, and an outbreak of smallpox, Posey's detachment arrived in South Carolina intact and in good spirits.[18] General Greene ordered Posey to march to Georgia and join General Anthony Wayne's small force outside of Savannah. The Virginians arrived on April 7th and were

---

[15] Posey, 88
[16] "Col. Thomas Posey to Col. Davies, 17 February, 1782", *Calendar of State Papers, Vol. 3*, 67
[17] "Col. Christian Febiger to Col. Davies, 23 February, 1782", *Calendar of State Papers, Vol. 3*, 72
[18] John Thornton Posey, 91-92

warmly greeted.[19]   Although Colonel Posey's detachment nearly doubled General Wayne's force, they were still significantly outnumbered by the British in Savannah.   The most General Wayne could do was harass enemy forage parties.[20]

In late June, it was General Wayne's corps that was suddenly harassed when 300 Creek warriors attacked in the middle of the night. They approached the Americans from the rear and stormed into camp undetected. Colonel Posey gave a detailed account of the battle to Henry Lee years later:

When the attack was made, it was with such fury and violence, at a dead time of the night when the men were in profound sleep (except the guards), with yelling and the use of their tomahawk, spears, scalping-knives, and guns, that our men were thrown into disorder.   Wayne and Posey had thrown their cloaks about them and lay down close to each other, the alarm soon roused them, and they had proceeded but a few steps when Captain Parker met Colonel Posey, and informing him that the suddenness of the attack had confused his men, wished to know if the colonel had any particular orders.   Posey immediately ordered that the light infantry should be rallied behind the house, and his exertions, united with Parker's, in a short space of time collected the men.

Posey then...ordered a charge through the enemy to the regiment; the charge was made with celerity and firmness, though the conflict was severe, many of the Indians falling by the force of the bayonet.   One or more of the enemy fell by Posey's own arm, and unfortunately for Sergeant Thompson of Parker's

---

[19] Ibid., 93
[20] John Thornton Posey,   93-94

light infantry (who contrary to orders had taken off his coat and tied up his head with a handkerchief, but who was manfully engaged, and had immediately next to Posey fired at an Indian, Posey took him, from his appearance with his coat off and head tied up, for an Indian, and thrusting his sword through his body, laid him at his feet...General Wayne filed off to the left where he fell in with a considerable body of Indians, and compelled them to retreat after a severe conflict. Thus, with the united force and much bravery of both officers and soldiers, the whole of the Indians were defeated and routed.[21]

This was the last significant military engagement of the Revolutionary War. The British evacuated Savannah less than a month after the battle, and by August, Colonel Posey and his men were outside Charleston with General Greene's army.[22] It was only a matter of months before the British left Charleston, as well. On December 14th, 1782, General Greene gave Colonel Posey the honor of leading the American army into the abandoned city.[23] The war was over.

Colonel Posey returned to Virginia during the winter and, on March 10th, 1783, resigned his commission in the continental army.[24] Seven years of distinguished military service were over. Ahead lay thirty-five more years of public service in Virginia, Kentucky, Louisiana, and Indiana.

---

[21] Lee, 558-559
[22] John Thornton Posey, 101
[23] Ibid., 102
[24] Ibid.

Epilogue

Shortly after the Revolutionary War, Thomas Posey moved to Spotsylvania County with a new wife and his two boys. He was appointed County Lieutenant and Magistrate, and served for nearly a decade. In 1793, President Washington appointed Posey to the rank of Brigadier General, and he served with General Anthony Wayne in the west. Posey eventually settled in Kentucky, where he became Speaker of the State Senate and Lieutenant Governor. He was also appointed Major-General of the state militia.

In 1810 Posey moved to the Louisiana Territory. Two years later, he was appointed to the United States Senate to represent the newly created state of Louisiana. In 1813, President Madison appointed Posey Governor of the Indiana Territory, and he once again relocated to the west. It was in Indiana, in 1818, that Thomas Posey passed away, at the age of sixty-eight.[25]

---

[25] Posey Biography and John Thornton Posey
  Note: For a much more in depth account of Thomas Posey's life, see John Thornton Posey, *General Thomas Posey: Son of the American Revolution*, East Lansing: Michigan State Univ. Press, 1992

Bibliography

Books

Baxter, James ed. *The British Invasion from the North: Digby's Journal of the Campaigns of Generals Carleton and Burgoyne from Canada, 1776-1777.* New York: Da Capo Press, 1970.

Boatner III, Mark M. *Encyclopedia of the American Revolution.* 3rd ed., Stanpole Books, 1994.

Bodle, Wayne, *The Valley Forge Winter: Civilians and Soldiers in War.* PA: Pennsylvania State University Press, 2002.

Borick, Carl P. *A Gallant Defense: The Siege of Charleston, 1780.* University of South Carolina Press, 2003

Boyd, Julian, ed. *The Papers Thomas Jefferson.* Vol. 3-6, Princeton, NJ: Princeton University Press, 1951.

Boyle, Joseph Lee. *Writings from the Valley Forge Encampment of the Continental Army.* Vol. 1-2 Bowie:Heritage Books Inc.,2000.

Brown, Lloyd A. & Howard H. Peckman ed. *Revolutionary War Journals of Henry Dearborn: 1775-1783.* Freeport, NY: Books for Libraries Press, 1939.

Burgoyne, John. *A State of the Expedition from Canada.* New York Times & Arno Press, 1969.

Campbell, Charles *The Orderly Book of that Portion of the American Army stationed at or near Williamsburg, Virginia under the command of General Andrew Lewis, from March 18th, 1776 to August 20th, 1776.* Richmond, VA: 1860.

Carrington, Henry B. *Battles of the American Revolution.* New York: A. S. Barnes & Co., 1877.

Cecere, Michael. *An Officer of Very Extraordinary Merit: Charles Porterfield and the American War for Independence, 1775-1780.* Westminster, MD: Heritage Books, 2004

Cecere, Michael. *They Behaved Like Soldiers: Captain John Chilton and the Third Virginia Regiment.* Westminster, MD: Heritage Books, 2004

Chase, Philander D. ed. *The Papers of George Washington: Revolutionary War Series.* Charlottesville: University Press of Virginia, 2000.

Clark, William, ed. *Naval Documents of the American Revolution, Vol. 5.* Washington: 1970.

Commager, Henry and Richard Morris, ed. "Journal of Captain Allen McLane, 15 July, 1779", *The Spirit of 'Seventy-Six: The Story of the American Revolution as Told by Participants.* NY: Castle Books, 1967.

Conrad, Dennis M. *The Papers of General Nathanael Greene.* Vol. 9-11, Chapel Hill: University of North Carolina Press, 1997-2000.

Cresswell, Nicholas. *Journal of Nicholas Cresswell: 1774-1777.* New York: The Dial Press, 1924.

Cullen, Charles and Herbert Johnson, ed. *The Papers of John Marshall.* Vol. 1, Chapel Hill : Univ. of NC Press, 1974

Dann, John C. *The Revolution Remembered: Eyewitness Accounts of the War Independence.* Chicago: University of Chicago Press, 1980.

Dawson, Henry B. "General Daniel Morgan: An Autobiography" *The Historical Magazine and Notes and Queries Concerning the Antiquities, History and Biography of America.* 2nd Series, Vol. 9, Morrisania, NY, 1871.

Dorman, John Frederick. *Virginia Revolutionary Pension Applications, Volumes 1-52.* Washington D.C., 1958-1995.

Ewald, Captain Johann. *Diary of the American War: A Hessian Journal.* New Haven: Yale Univ. Press, 1979. Translated & edited by Joseph Tustin

Fitzpatrick, John C. *The Writings of George Washington from the Original Manuscripts, 1745-1799.* Washington: U.S. Govt. Printing Office, 1931.

Graham, James. *The Life of General Daniel Morgan.* Bloomingburg, NY: Zebrowski Historical Services, 1993.

Greene, Jack P. *The Diary of Landon Carter of Sabine Hall, 1752-1778: Volume 1-2*. Charlottesville: University Press of Virginia, 1965.

Greenman, Jeremiah. *Diary of a Common Soldier in the American Revolution, 1775-1783*. DeKalb, IL: Northern Illinois University Press, 1978 Edited by Robert C. Bray and Paul E. Bushnell

Hening, William *The Statutes at Large Being a Collection of all the Laws of Virginia, Vol. 9*. Richmond: J & G Cochran, 1821.

Higginbotham, Don. *Daniel Morgan: Revolutionary Rifleman*. Chapel Hill: Univeristy of North Carolina Press, 1961

Hinrichs, Captain Johann. *The Siege of Charleson: Diaries and Letters of Hessian Officers*. Ann Arbor: University of Michigan Press, 1938. Trans. & ed. Bernhard A. Uhlendorf,

Jackman, Sydney ed. *With Burgoyne from Quebec: An Account of the Life at Quebec and of the Famous Battle at Saratoga.* Toronto: Macmillan of Canada, 1963.
Note: First published as volume one of Travels Through the Interior Parts of North America, by Thomas Anburey

Johnson, Henry. *The Storming of Stony Point on the Hudson, Midnight, July 15, 1779: Its Importance in the Light of Unpublished Documents.* New York: James T. White, 1900.

Kapp, Friedrich. *The Life of Frederick William von Steuben.* NY: Corner House Historical Publications, 1999 (Originally published in 1859)

LaCrosse Jr., Richard B. The Frontier Rifleman. Union City, TN: Pioneer Press, 1989.

LaCrosse Jr., Richard B. *Revolutionary Rangers: Daniel Morgan's Riflemen and Their Role on the Northern Frontier.* Bowie, MD: Heritage Books, 2002.

Lamb, Roger. *An Original and Authentic Journal of Occurrences During the Late American War from Its Commencement to 1783.* Dublin: Wilkinson & Courtney, 1809.

Lee, Charles. *The Lee Papers, Vol. 1.* Collections of the New York Historical Society, 1871.

Lee, Henry. *The Revolutionary War Memoirs of General Henry Lee.* New York: Da Capo Press, 1998. Originally Published in 1812

Lee, Nell Moore. *Patriot Above Profit: A Portrait of Thomas Nelson, Jr.* Nashville, TN: Rutledge Hill Press, 1988.

Lesser, Charles H. ed. *The Sinews of Independence: Monthly Strength Reports of the Continental Army.* Chicago: The Univiversity of Chicago Press, 1976.

Loprieno, Don. *The Enterprise in Contemplation: The Midnight Assault of Stony Point.* Westminster MD: Heritage Books, 2004.

Lowell, Edward J. *Letters and Memoirs Relating to the War of American Independence and the Capture of the German Troops at Saratoga.* Williamstown, MA: Corner House Publishers, 1975.

Luzader, John. *Decision on the Hudson: The Battles of Saratoga.* Eastern National, 2002.

Marshall, John. *The Life of George Washington Vol. 2.* Fredericksburg, VA: The Citizens' Guild of Washington's Boyhood Home, 1926.

Martin, David. *The Philadelphia Campaign, June 1777 – July 1778.* Da Capa Press, 1993.

McGuire, Thomas. *The Surprise of Germantown, October 4, 1777.* Cliveden of the National Trust for Historic Preservation and Thomas Publications, 1994.

McIlwaine, H.R. ed. *Journals of the Council of the State of Virginia, Vol. 1.* Richmond: Virginia State Library, 1931.

Morrissey, Brendan. *Saratoga 1777: Turning Point of the Revolution.* Osprey Publishing, 2000.

Moore, Frank. *Diary of the American Revolution, from Newspapers and Original Documents.* 2 vols. New York:Charles Schibner, 1860. Reprint. New York: New York Times & Arno Press, 1969.

Mowday, Bruce E. *September 11, 1777, Washington's Defeat at Brandywine Dooms Philadelphia.* Shippensburg, PA: White Mane Books, 2002.

O'Kelly, Patrick. *Nothing But Blood and Slaughter: The Revolutionary War in the Carolinas*. Blue House Tavern Press, 2004.

Palmer, William ed. *Calendar of Virginia State Papers.* Vol. 1-2, Richmond: R.F. Walker, 1875.

Posey, John Thornton. *General Thomas Posey: Son of the American Revolution*. East Lansing: Michigan State Univ. Press, 1992.

Pausch, George. *Journal of Captain Pausch, Chief of the Hanau Artillery During the Burgoyne Campaign*. Albany, NY: Joel Munsell's Sons, 1886. Translated by William L. Stone.

Reed, John F. *Campaign to Valley Forge: July 1, 1777 – December 19, 1777*. Pioneer Press, 1980.

Riedesel, Madam. Letters and Memoirs Relating to the War of American Independence and the Capture of the German Troops at Saratoga. New York: G. & C. Carvill, 1827.

Rogers, Horatio ed. *Hadden's Journal and Orderly Book: A Journal Kept in Canada and Upon Burgoyne's Campaign in 1776 and 1777*. Boston: Gregg Press, 1972.

Russell, T. Tripplett and John K. Gott. <u>Fauquier County in the Revolution.</u> Westminster, MD : Willow Bend Books, 1988.

Saffell, W.T.R. *Records of the Revolutionary War*, 3rd ed. Baltimore: Charles Saffell, 1894.

Scheer, George F., and Hugh F. Rankin. *Rebels &
Redcoats: The American Revolution through the Eyes
of Those Who Fought and Lived It.* New York: Da
Capo Press, 1987.

Selby, John E. *The Revolution in Virginia : 1775-1783.*
New York : Holt Inc., 1996.

Sellers, John R. *The Virginia Continental Line.*
Williamsburg: The Virginia Bicentennial Commission,
1978.

Simcoe, Lt. Col. John. *Simcoe's Military Jouirnal: A History*
of the Operations of a Partisan Corps Called the
Queen's Rangers, Commanded by Lieut. Col. J. G.
Simcoe, During *the War of Revolution.* New York:
New York Times and Arno Press, 1968.

Sanchez-Saavedra, E.M. *A Guide to Virginia Military
Organizations in the American Revolution, 1774-
1787.* Westminster, MD: Willow Bend Books, 1978.

Smith, Jean Edward. *John Marshall : Definer of a Nation.*
New York : Holt Inc., 1996.

Smith, Samuel. *The Battle of Brandywine.* Monmouth Beach,
NJ: Philip Freneau Press, 1976.

Sparks, Jared ed. *The Correspondence of the American
Revolution being Letters of Eminent Men to George
Washington.* Vol. 2, Boston : Little, Brown & Co.,
1853.

Stewart , Catesby Willis. *The Life of Brigadier General William Woodford of The American Revolution.* Vol. 2, Richmond, VA: Whittet & Shepperson, 1973.

Stille, Charles. *Major-General Anthony Wayne and the Pennsylvania Line in the Continental Army.* Port Washington, NY: Kenniket Press, Inc., 1968. First published in 1893

Stryker, William. *The Battle of Monmouth.* Princeton: Princeton University Press, 1927.

Symonds, Craig L. *A Battlefield ATLAS of the American Revolution.* The Nautical & Aviation Publishing Co. of America Inc., 1986.

Taaffe, Stephen R. *The Philadelphia Campaign, 1777-1778.* University of Kansas Press, 2003.

Tarleton, Banastre. *A History of the Campaigns of 1780-1781 in the Southern Provinces of North America.* NH: AYER Company, 1999. Originally printed in 1787

Tarter, Brent and Robert Scribner, ed. *Revolutionary Virginia: The Road to Independence, Vol. 1-7.* University Press of Virginia, 1983.

Thacher, James. *A Military Journal during the American Revolutionary War.* Hartford: CT, S. Andrus and Son, 1854. Reprint, New York: Arno Press, 1969.

Tharp, Louise Hall. *The Baroness and the General.* Boston: Little, Brown & Co., 1962.

Townsend, Joseph. "Some Account of the British Army under the Command of General Howe, and of the Battle of Brandywine," *Eyewitness Accounts of the American Revolution.* New York: Arno Press, 1969.

Uhlendorf, Bernhard A. ed. & trans. *The Siege of Charleston: With an Account of the Province of South Carolina: Diaries and Letters of Hessian Officers.* Ann Arbor, MI: University of Michigan Press, 1938.

Wilkinson, James. *Memoirs of My Own Times, Vol. 1* Philadelphia: Abraham Small, 1816 *Reprinted by AMS Press Inc., :NY, 1973*

Ward, Christopher. *The Delaware Continentals, 1776-1783.* Wilmington, DE: History Society of Delaware, 1941.

Ward, Harry M. *Duty, Honor, or Country : General George Weedon and the American Revolution.* Philadelphia : American Philosophical Society, 1979.

Wasmus, J.F. *An Eyewitness Account of the American Revolution and New England Life: The Journal of J.F. Wasmus, German Company Surgeon, 1776-1783.* NY: Greenwood Press, 1990. Translated by Helga Doblin

Willard, Margaret. ed., *Letters of the American Revolution: 1774-1776.* Boston & New York: Houghton Mifflin Co., 1925

Wright, Robert K. *The Continental Army.* Washington, D.C. Center of Military History: United States Army, 1989.

Wrike, Peter. *The Governor's Island.* Gwynn, VA: The Gwynn's Island Museum, 1993.

Periodicals

Boyle, Joseph Lee. "From Saratoga to Valley Forge: The Diary of Lt. Samuel Armstrong," *The Pennsylvania Magazine of History and Biography,* Vol. 121, No. 3 July 1997

Dearborn, Henry. "A Narrative of the Saratoga Campaign – Major General Henry Dearborn, 1815, *The Bulletin of the Fort Ticonderoga Museum.* Vol. 1 no. 5, January, 1929.

Elmer, Ebenezer. "The Journal of Ebenezer Elmer," *The Pennsylvania Magazine of History and Biography.* Vol. 35 Philadelphia: Historical Society of Pennsylvania, 1911.

McMichael, James. "The Diary of Lt. James McMichael of the Pennsylvania Line, 1776-1778," *The Pennsylvania Magazine of History and Biography.* Vol. 16, no. 2, 1892.

Montresor, John. "Journal of Captain John Montresor," *The Pennsylvania Magazine of History and Biography.* Vol. 5, 1881

Schnitzer, Eric. "Battling for the Saratoga Landscape", *Cultural Landscape Report: Saratoga Battle, Saratoga National Park,* Vol. 1, Boston, MA: Olmsted Center for Landscape Preservation.

Sullivan, Thomas. "Before and After the Battle of
    Brandywine: Extracts from the Journal of Sergeant
    Thomas Sullivan of H.M. Forty-Ninth Regiment of
    Foot," *The Pennsylvania Magazine of History and
    Biography.* Vol 31, Philadelphia: Historical Society of
    Pennsylvania, 1907.

Tyler, Lyon. "The Old Virginia Line in the Middle States
    During the American Revolution," *Tyler's Quarterly
    Historical and Genealogical Magazine: Vol.12.*
    Richmond, VA: Richmond Press Inc., 1931.

"The Actions at Brandywine and Paoli, Described by a British
    Officer," *The Pennsylvania Magazine of History and
    Biography.* Vol. 24, Philadelphia: Historical Society of
    Pennsylvania, 1905.

Unpublished Works

Brigadier General George Weedon's Correspondence Account
    of the Battle of Brandywine, 11 September, 1777. The
    original manuscript is in the collections of the Chicago
    Historical Society, Transcribed by Bob McDonald,
    2001.

Heth, William. "Orderly Book of Major William Heth of the
    Third (sic) Virginia Regiment, May 15 – July 1,
    1777", *Virginia Historical Society Collections.* New
    Series, 11 1892.
    Note: This orderly book is incorrectly titled and is actually the
    orderly book of Daniel Morgan's 11th Virginia Regiment.

Lt. Col. Richard Butler to Col. James Wilson, 22 January,
    1778 Gratz Collection, Case 4, Box 11, Historical
    Society of Pennsylvania.

The Orderly Book of Captain Robert Gamble of the Second
Virginia Regiment, Commanded by Colonel Christian
Febiger, August 21 – November 16, 1779
Accessed via www.ls.net/~newriver/va/gamble1.html

Posey, Thomas. "*A Short Biography of the Life of Governor
Thomas Posey*," Thomas Posey Papers. Indiana
Historical Society Library, Indianapolis, IN.

Posey, Thomas, *Revolutionary War Journal*,
Thomas Posey Papers, Indiana Historical
Society Library, Indianapolis, IN

Index

About the Author

Michael Cecere Sr. is the proud father of two wonderful children, Jenny and Michael Jr., and the grateful husband of Susan Cecere. He teaches American History at Robert E. Lee High School in Fairfax County, Virginia (full-time) and at Northern Virginia Community College (part-time). He holds a Master of Arts Degree from the University of Akron in History and another in Political Science. An avid Revolutionary and Civil War re-enactor, he is a member of the 3rd and 7th Virginia Regiments and the Liberty Rifles, and participates in numerous living history events throughout the year. *Captain Thomas Posey and the 7th Virginia Regiment* is his third book. His first two, entitled, *They Behaved Like Soldiers: Captain John Chilton and the Third Virginia Regiment,* and *An Officer of Very Extraordinary Merit: Charles Porterfield and the American War for Independence, 1775-1780,* both provide insight into the lives of the officers and their units. He is currently conducting research on the American Rifleman in the Revolutionary War.

www.ingramcontent.com/pod-product-compliance
Lightning Source LLC
Chambersburg PA
CBHW060656100426
42734CB00047B/2008